LOUISE CHANDLER MOULTON

Louise Chandler Moulton, ÆT. 20

Frontispiece

LOUISE CHANDLER MOULTON

Poet and Friend

BY

LILIAN WHITING

BOSTON

LITTLE, BROWN, AND COMPANY

1910

Printers
S. J. PARKHILL & CO., BOSTON, U. S. A.

CONTENTS

ILLUSTRATIONS

LOUISE CHANDLER MOULTON

POET AND FRIEND

CHAPTER I

1835–1853

The poet in a golden clime was born
    With golden stars above. — TENNYSON.

The lingering charm of a dream that is fled. — L. C. M.

GENIUS, love, and friendship make up a triple dower which holds within itself the possibilities of high destiny. Their changing combinations comprise all intensities of human joy and human sorrow: the richness of sympathetic companionship; the enchantments of romance; the glow and passion of artistic achievement; and that power of initiating noble service which invests life with the

loveliness of perfect deeds
More strong than all poetic thought.

In few lives have these possibilities been more fully realized than in that of Louise Chandler Moulton, poet and friend, and

lover of the beautiful. Poet born and poet
made, she developed her natural lyric gift
into a rare mastery of poetic art. She wore
her singing-robes with an unconscious grace,
and found in her power of song the determin-
ing influence which colored and shaped her
life. Her lyrics were the spontaneous expression, the natural out-pouring, of a lofty and
beautiful spirit. Her poetic instinct radiated
in her ardent and generous sympathies, her
exquisite interpretations of sentiment and
feeling; it informed all her creative work
with a subtle charm pervasive as the fragrance of a rose. Her artistic impulse was,
indeed, the very mainspring of her life; it expressed itself not only in the specific forms of
lyrics and of prose romance, but in her varied
range of friendships and in her intense and
discriminating love of literature. Mrs. Moulton was not of the order of the poet who

> puts what he hath of poetry in his verse
> And leaves none for his life.

Her life as well as her art expressed her gift of
song. She was a poet not only in singing, but
no less in living. Her friendships were singularly wide and eclectic, determined always
from the inner vision. They were the friendships of mutual recognition and of sympathetic

ministry. Her tenderness of feeling responded to every human need. Others might turn away from the unattractive; to her the simple fact that kindness was needed was a claim which she could not deny.

This was the more striking from the fact that from her early girlhood her gifts, her culture, and her personal charm won recognition in the most brilliant circles. To be as unconsciously gracious to peasant as to prince was in her very nature. Thomas Wentworth Higginson, alluding to Mrs. Moulton's social prestige in London, wrote:

" . . . It is pleasant to feel that she owes this result quite as much to her qualities of character as to her gifts of intellect. There never lived, perhaps, a more thoroughly open-hearted and generous woman; and the poorest and least gifted applicant might always seek her as successfully as the most famous and influential."

This symmetry of character, a certain fine balance of the gifts of mind and heart, was the natural outcome, it may be, of a worthy ancestry. So far as is known, the Chandlers lived originally in Hampshire, England, where, in the sixteenth century, arms were granted to them. Many of these Chandlers were men distinguished in their day. In 1887 was commemorated at Philadelphia the two hundredth anniversary of the arrival in this country of one of the first Chandlers known to have immigrated. This was a follower of Fox, who fled from persecution, and settled in Pennsylvania. A group of ten English Puritans settled long before the Revolution in what was afterward the township of Pomfret, Connecticut: and from one of these was descended Lucius Chandler, the father of Louise. The Chandler family throughout gave evidence of decided intellectual ability, and this was strengthened by marriages with other sound Puritan stock. Through her paternal grandmother Mrs. Moulton was descended from the Rev. Aaron Cleveland, of literary reputation in the late eighteenth century, and of account in his day as a wit. This relationship linked her in remote cousinship with Edmund Clarence Stedman, a tie which both cherished. The two poets congratulated themselves on a common great-grandmother who was a classical scholar, famed for her familiarity with Greek.

Lucius L. Chandler married Louisa Rebecca Clark, also of good English ancestry. Mrs. Chandler has been described by Harriet Prescott Spofford as "a gentle, gracious

Elmwood Cottage, Pomfret, Conn., the Girlhood Home
of Louise Chandler Moulton

Page 5

woman, a noted beauty in her youth, but
singularly free from the vanity and selfishness
of most noted beauties." The only surviving
child of this marriage was born at Pomfret on
April 10, 1835, and was christened Ellen
Louise. Mr. Chandler's farm lay on the
edge of the quiet Connecticut town, the land-
scape pleasantly diversified by adjacent hills
and forests, and the modest, comfortable
home was surrounded by flowers and trees.
In later years, recalling her childhood, Mrs.
Moulton wrote:

> My thoughts go home to that old brown house
>   With its low roof sloping down to the east,
> And its garden fragrant with roses and thyme
> That blossom no longer except in rhyme,
>   Where the honey-bees used to feast.
>
> Afar in the west the great hills rose,
>   Silent and steadfast, and gloomy and gray.
> I thought they were giants, and doomed to keep
> Their watch while the world should wake or sleep,
>   Till the trumpet should sound on the judgment-day.
>
> And I was as young as the hills were old,
>   And the world was warm with the breath of spring;
> And the roses red and the lilies white
> Budded and bloomed for my heart's delight,
>   And the birds in my heart began to sing.

A winsome little sprite seems Ellen Louise
to have been, revealing, even in her earliest
years, a quaint touch of her father's courtly
dignity combined with her mother's refine-

which may easily be accepted by those who have in memory the clear, soft speech of Mrs. Moulton. Often was she playfully entreated to

> lend to the rhyme of the poet
> The music of thy voice;

the lines seeming almost to have been written to describe her recital of poetry.

The fairies who came to the christening of this golden-haired and golden-voiced child seemed, indeed, to have given her all good gifts in full measure. She was endowed with beauty and with genius; she was born into surroundings of liberal comfort and of refinement; into prosperity which made possible the gratification of all reasonable desires and aspirations of a gifted girl. It was her fortune through life to be sheltered from material anxieties. To a nature less sensitively perceptive of the needs and sorrows of others, to one less generous and tender, the indulgence which fell to her as an only and idolized child, might have fostered that indifference to the condition of those less favored which deprives its possessor of the richest experiences of life. With her to see need or misfortune was to feel the instant impulse to relieve or at least to alleviate the suffering. Colonel Higginson, in recalling her life in England said:

" I shall never forget, in particular, with
what tears in his eyes the living representative of Philip Bourke Marston spoke to me
in London of her generous self-devotion to his
son, the blind poet, of whom she became the
editor and biographer."

Emerson has declared that comforts and
advantages are good if one does not use them
as a cushion on which to go to sleep. With
Mrs. Moulton her native gifts seemed to gen-
erate aspiration and effort for noble achievement.

Among the schoolmates of her childish
years was the boy who was afterward the
artist Whistler, who was one year her senior.
As children they often walked home from
school together, and one night the little girl
was bewailing that she could not draw a map
like the beautiful one he had displayed to an
admiring group that day. It was a gorgeous
creation in colored crayons, an "arrangement" that captivated the village school with
much the same ardor that the future artist
was destined to inspire from the art connois-
seurs of two continents. A sad object, indeed,
was the discordant affair that Ellen Louise
held up in self-abasement and hopelessness
while she poured out her enthusiasm on his

achievement. The lad received this praise with lofty scorn. "That's nothing," he exclaimed; "you think this is anything? Take it; I don't want it; you just see what I can do to-morrow! I'll bring you then something worth talking about." And with the precious trophy in her possession, the little girl made her way home. True to his word, the next morning "Jimmy" brought her a package whose very wrapping revealed the importance of its contents; and when she had breathlessly opened it, there was disclosed an exquisite little painting. Under a Gothic arch that breathed — no one knew what enchanted hints of "the glory that was Greece and the grandeur that was Rome," or some far-away dreams of Venice, or other dimly prefigured marvel in the child's fancy, was an old monk; through the picture were silver gleams, and a vague glint of purple, and altogether, it held some far prophecy of the brilliant future yet undisclosed. All her life Mrs. Moulton kept the gift. It had an unobtrusive place in her drawing-room, and even figured modestly at the great Whistler exhibition which was held in Boston by the Copley Society after the death of the artist.

In some ways Ellen Louise had a rather lonely childhood save that an imaginative and poetic nature peoples a world of its own. The little girl had, as it chanced, no playmates near at hand to supply the place of brothers and sisters; and her companions were those that fancy created. In later years she wrote of this period:

"I never felt alone. Dream children companioned me, and were as real to my thoughts as if other eyes than my own could have seen them. Their sorrows saddened me, their mirth amused me, they shared my visions, my hopes; and the strange dread with which I — brought up in a Puritan household where election and predestination were familiar words — looked forward to the inevitable end.

"Yet haunted as I was by the phantom future, I was happy in the present. I am afraid I was what is called a spoiled child. I loved horses and I loved verses, and on my eighth birthday two presents were made me — a well-equipped saddle horse, and a book of poems. The horse ran away with me that same afternoon while my too sociable father, who was riding with me, stopped to talk town politics with a neighbor; but my steed raced homeward, and I reached my own door in safety. The book of verse I have yet. It was by Mrs. Hemans — now so cruelly forgotten."

Her imaginative nature showed itself in many ways. She says:

" I was not allowed to read fiction or to play any but the most serious games. . . . Hence I was thrown upon my own resources for amusement. I remember when I was only eight years old carrying in my head all the summer a sort of Spanish drama, as I called it, though I knew little of Spain except some high-sounding Spanish names which I gave to my characters. Each day, as soon as I could get away by myself, I summoned these characters as if my will had been a sort of invisible call-boy, and then watched them performing. It did not seem to me that I created them, but rather that I summoned them, and their behavior often astonished me. For one of them, a young girl, who obstinately persisted in dying of consumption, I sincerely grieved."

She had written from the age of seven verses which would hardly have discredited her maturer years. A stanza written when she was nine runs:

> Autumn is a pleasant time
> Breathing beauty in our clime;
> Even its flowerets breathe of love
> Which is sent us from above.

The lines seem to have written themselves, but as Autumn had been assigned as a theme-subject at school she dealt with it also in prose. She began with the assertion: "Autumn to the contemplative mind is the loveliest season of the year"; and closed with the rather startling line: "All these are beautiful, but let us leave the contemplation of them until another winter dawns on the languid sea of human life." One almost wonders that under a training which permitted English so florid Mrs. Moulton was able to develop her admirable style. At ten she was writing "An Address to the Ocean" and a meditation on "Hope." Another effort was "The Bell of My Native City," and this she explained in a footnote as an imaginative composition, composed to express the feelings of an exile who had been "unjustly banished from his country." She was taken a few months later on a little trip to "Tribes Hill" on the Mohawk, and in a "History of My Journey Home from Tribes Hill" records gravely:

" It was a beautiful September morning that ushered in the day of my departure. I rose with the first dawning of light to gaze once more upon those scenes whose loveliness I had so loved to trace. I rejoiced to pay a tribute of gratitude to some of the many friends whose society had contributed so much to my happiness when away from the home of my childhood. . . . At noon I started. . . . For many a mile, as we were drawn with dazzling rapidity by our wild steam horse (whose voice resounded like the rolling of distant thunder), I could catch glimpses of the dark blue waters of the Mohawk, which I had so loved to gaze upon, and to whose music I had so often listened in the hush of evening, from my open window, or when walking on its green banks with a friend, dearly loved and highly prized, but whom I shall, perhaps, meet no more forever. . . . As I rode along my thoughts reverted to her. The river gleaming in quiet beauty from beneath the green foliage of its fringing trees reminded me of the hours we had spent together in contemplating it. The excitement of travelling and the loved home to which I was hastening were alike forgotten in these reveries of the past."

A sentence of more than a hundred and fifty words that follows quite graphically depicts a walk taken with this friend, and the child continued:

"From such reveries of the past was I awakened by the stopping of the cars at Albany. That night we embarked on board a steamboat, and as we glided o'er the Hudson river, my heart bounded with delight. I stood alone before an open window, and my soul drank in the richness of the scene."

One can but smile at this rhapsody of the child of eleven, but it is after all suggestive of literary powers genuine if undeveloped. It shows, too, a nature sensitive to beauty and a heart full of quick responsiveness to friendship. The gifts of the woman are foreshadowed even in the extravagances of the girl.

The blank books in which Louise recorded her impressions and thoughts and copied out her verses in the years between eight and eighteen afford material for a curious study of unfolding tendencies. A religious meeting to which she is taken suggests a long dissertation on "The Missionary;" and this sketch assumes an imaginative form. The missionary and his bride are described as voyaging over the ocean to the field of his labors in these terms:

" . . . But when they had entirely lost sight of land Charles clasped his loved one to his heart and whispered, 'Be comforted, dearest;

we go not alone, for is not He with us who said, "Lo, I am with thee always, even unto the end of the world!"' . . . The young bride burst into an agony of tears. . . . Her husband led her on deck, and showed her the sun's last, golden rays that lay upon the waves, sparkling like a thousand brilliants. . . . It seemed a sea of burning gold. . . . A high and holy resolve rose in the hearts of the young missionaries. . . . They had left a circle of brilliant acquaintances for the untutored heathen. . . . They left the deck to sit down in a quiet nook and read the word of Him for whom they forsook all earthly pleasures."

Not only do the note-books give such hints of the future story-teller, but they abound in verse. It is noticeable that although much of this is crude and inevitably childish, it is yet remarkably free from false measures. The child had been gifted by heaven with an ear wonderfully true. The books contain also many quotations copied from the volumes she was from time to time reading. Moore, Mrs. Hemans, Tupper, Willis, Longfellow, Whittier, Campbell, are among the names found here most frequently. Curiously enough the record shows no trace of Scott, of Byron, of Wordsworth, or of Coleridge.

One of the felicitous orderings of her school-days was that which placed her as a pupil of the Rev. Roswell Park, the Episcopal rector in Pomfret, and Principal of a school called Christ Church Hall. Here she easily carried off the honors when "compositions" were required.

"Will Miss Ellen Louise Chandler please remain a moment after the school is dismissed," was the disconcerting request of the teacher one day.

The purpose of the interview was a private inquiry where the girl had "found" the poem which she had read in the literary exercises of the afternoon.

"Why, I can't tell," she answered; "it all wrote itself from my own mind."

The instructor looked at her earnestly for a moment, — this dainty young girl with the rose-flush deepening in her sweet face, — and replied: "Then I sincerely congratulate you." And she went on her way.

The commonplace books of her thirteenth year, kept while she was still a pupil at this school, show more clearly than ever the dawning power of the young poet. Her reading was not indiscriminate, but selective, inclining almost equally to poetry and to serious prose. Of the usual schoolgirl love of novels

day. It is as admirably typical of the fashion
of the day as the bonnets of the forties which
one finds in a dusty attic.

> Hush thy footfall, lightly tread;
> Passing by a loved one's bed.
> Dust hath gathered on her brow,
> Silently she resteth now.
>
> Sank she into dreamless rest
> Clasping rosebuds to her breast;
> With her forehead pale and fair
> 'Neath the midnight of her hair.
>
> . . . .
>
> There we laid her down to sleep
> Where the wild flowers o'er her weep.
> Earth below and blue sky o'er,
> Sweetly sleeps our own Lenore.

Another lyric, written about this time to
Governor Cleveland on the death of his only
daughter, contained these lines:

> What time she braided up her hair
>   With summer buds and sprays of flowers,
> It was as if some saint had shed
>   Heaven's light on this dim world of ours;
> And kneeling where her feet have trod,
>   We watched to see the glory break
> When angel fingers at the dawn
>   Heaven's portals opened for her sake.

Of these lines Edmund Clarence Stedman
wrote with youthful enthusiasm:

"This is almost equal to the picture of Madeline in 'The Eve of St. Agnes,' as she kneels before the oriel window of the casement, high and triple-arched, in all the holiness of prayer."

The stories which the young writer contributed to the gift-books bore the most startling titles: "Inez Caisco; or, The Flower of Catalonia"; "Beatrice; or, The Beautiful Tambourine Girl"; "Evilia; or, The Enchantress." Of Isabel Sydenham, the heroine of one of these tales, it is told that she "threw open her casement," — no self-respecting story-teller of the mid-century called a window anything but a casement, — and sighed: "If he were only here, how we might enjoy the surpassing loveliness!" Of this sensitive creature, who naturally "yearns" for all sorts of impossible things, her creator remarks that "ideality was the predominating characteristic of her mind." According to gift-book standards no heroine could be more eminently satisfactory.

Not content with being a contributor to the annuals of others, Miss Chandler compiled a gift-book of her own: "The Book of the Boudoir; a Gift for All Seasons, Edited by Ellen Louise." By her publisher's insistence

" I remember that the Calvinistic doctrines I was taught filled my imagination with an awful foreboding of doom and despair. I can recall waking in the depth of the night, cold with horror, and saying to myself, 'Why, if I 'm not among the elect, I *can't* be saved, no matter how hard I try,' and stealing along on my little bare feet to my mother's bed, praying to be taken in, with a vague sense that if I must be lost in the far future, at least now I must go where love could comfort me, and human arms shelter me from the shapeless terrors that mocked my solitude."

While, however, the lack of a more encouraging interpretation of Divine Goodness undoubtedly was to a degree responsible for the minor chords which became habitual in her verse, the natural longing which is part of the poetic nature, was in Mrs. Moulton unusually strong and was exaggerated by the literary modes of her day. On the whole the influences of her childhood were sweet and sound and wholesome. Her natural love of beauty was fed and developed, her inherent literary taste was nourished by sympathy and by success, and her wonderful sensitiveness to literary form trained by early and constant practice. It is even possible that the very harshness of Calvinism, which was almost the only shadow, was a healthful influence which deepened and strengthened her art, that might without this have suffered from sunshine too uninterrupted.

CHAPTER II

1853–1860

A beautiful and happy girl
  With step as light as summer air. — WHITTIER.

Her glorious fancies come from far
Beneath the silver evening-star,
And yet her heart is ever near. — LOWELL.

At dawn of Love, at dawn of Life. — L. C. M.

IN a lyric written by Mrs. Moulton in after years, occurs the lovely line quoted above, which seems vividly to describe her as she stood, a girl of eighteen, on the threshold of a new phase of life.

Young as she was Miss Chandler had already, by her newspaper and magazine work, made for herself a reputation, and she now collected the papers which made up the volume spoken of in the previous chapter, "This, That, and the Other," with the encouraging result of a sale of twenty thousand copies. The *North American Review* was then almost the only magazine in the country exclusively devoted to criticism and the intellectual life. Much of the best literary

work of the time, in the way of fiction and
poetry, appeared in such periodicals as *Godey's
Lady's Book*, *Peterson's Magazine*, and the
like; and to these Miss Chandler was a constant contributor. The weekly newspapers
were rich in poems by Longfellow, Emerson,
Whittier, the Cary sisters, N. P. Willis, Poe,
and many others of permanent fame. Be-
sides these, a host of the transient singers of
the day, literary meteors, flitted across the
firmament, not unfrequently with some song
or story which individually was quite as
worthy of recognition as were those of their
contemporaries whose power to sustain themselves in longer flights and to make good the
early promise has earned their title to permanent recognition. Mrs. Moulton's scrapbooks
indicate how rich were the literary columns
of the newspapers in those days. There
being then no international copyright law,
the American editor enriched his page with
the latest poem of Browning, Tennyson,
Swinburne, or Mrs. Browning. Longfellow,
Whittier, Holmes, Dr. Parsons, Nora Perry,
William Winter, the Stoddards (Richard Henry and Elizabeth), N. P. Willis, Saxe, Mrs.
Stowe, Jean Ingelow, Miss Mulock, Aldrich,
and Mary Clemmer, are largely represented
in these old scrapbooks. Many fugitive

poems, too, appear, as the "Bertha" of Anne
Whitney, a poem well entitled to literary
immortality; the "Three Kisses of Farewell,"
by Saxe Holm; the "Unseen Spirits," by
Willis, a poem too little known; and Mr.
Aldrich's "The Unforgiven," excluded from
his later editions, but which contains those
beautiful lines:

In the East the rose of morning biddeth fair to blossom soon,
But it never, never blossoms in this picture; and the moon
Never ceases to be crescent, and the June is always June.

Miss Chandler's book was one of over four
hundred pages, illustrated by the famous Rouse
(whose portrait of Emerson has always been
so highly considered), and its fine engravings
and its binding of crimson cloth combined
to give it a sumptuous appearance. The
Springfield Republican gave it pleasant recognition in these words:

"The writings of a young girl still on the
threshold of life and still to be regarded as a
bright, incarnate promise,— her writings are
very graceful, very tender, and very beautiful, just what the flowers of life's spring
should be."

The young author dedicated her book to
her mother in tender phrase, and her artless
"Preface" was one to disarm any adverse view.

In after years Mrs. Moulton smilingly replied to some questions regarding her initiation into authorship:

"I remember the huge posters with which they placarded the walls, headed, 'Read this book and see what a girl of eighteen can do.' I think I had the grace to be a little shocked at these posters, but the reviews were so kind, and said such lovely things that — Ah! shall I ever be so happy again as when I read them!"

Edmund Clarence Stedman, who had just left Yale College and who, at the beginning of his literary career, was editing a country paper in Connecticut, greeted Miss Chandler's book with the ardent praise of youth and friendship; but these warm phrases of approval were also the almost unanimous expression of all the reviewers of the day. The twentieth century reader may smile at Mr. Stedman's youthful distrust of the "strong-minded woman," but his remarks are interesting. Of "This, That, and the Other," he wrote:

"'This, That, and the Other,' is a collection of prose sketches and verse from the pen of a young lady fast rising into a literary reputation; a reputation which, though it is achieved in no 'Uncle Tom' or 'Fanny Fern' mode, is no less sure than that of Mrs. Stowe, or Sara Payson Willis, and will be more substantial, in that the works on which it is founded are more classic and in better taste. . . . Miss Chandler is a native of Pomfret in this state, and every denizen of Connecticut should be proud of her talents. She is beautiful and interesting; her manners are in marked distinction from the forwardness of the strong-minded woman of the day. . . ."

Epes Sargent, in the *Boston Transcript,* said:

". . . The ladies have invaded the field of fiction and carried off its most substantial triumphs. Mrs. Stowe, Fanny Fern, and now another name, if the portents do not deceive us, is about to be added — that of Miss Chandler, who although the youngest of the band (she is not yet nineteen), is overflowing with genius and promise. Such tales as those of 'Silence Adams,' 'A Husking Party at Ryefield,' 'Agnes Lee,' and 'Only an Old Maid,' reveal the pathos, the beauty, the power, the depth and earnestness of emotion that Ellen Louise has the art of transfusing

into the humblest and most commonplace
details. . . . But Ellen Louise must not be
deceived by injudicious admiration. Her style,
purified, chastened and subdued, would lose
none of its attractiveness. She gives evidence
of too noble a habit of thought to desire the
success which comes of the hasty plaudits
of the hour."

The book reviewing of 1853 was apparently
not unlike the spelling of George Eliot's poor
Mr. Tulliver,—"a matter of private judgment."
For although the stories of Ellen Louise were
singularly sweet and winsome in their tone,
with an unusual grasp of sentiment and glow
of fancy for so youthful and inexperienced a
writer, they could yet hardly claim to rank
with the work of Mrs. Stowe. The leading
papers of that day united, however, in an
absolute chorus of praise for the young
author, who is pronounced "charming," and
"overflowing with talent"; the "refinement
and delicacy" of her work, her "rare maturity
of thought and style," and a myriad other
literary virtues were discerned and celebrated
to the extent that the resources of the language
of the country would allow. A sonnet was
written to her, signed "B. P. S.," which
signature is easily translated to us in these

days as that of B. P. Shillaber, the author of "Mrs. Partington." The sonnet is entitled:

TO ELLEN LOUISE

Take this, and that, and t' other all together,
  We like you better every day we 're breathing;
And round our hearts this pleasant summer weather
  Your fairy fingers deathless flowers are weaving:
We read delightedly your charming pages
  Fraught in each line with truth and magic beauty;
Here starts a tear that some hid woe assuages,
  And there is heard a voice that calls to duty.
And proudly may Connecticut, sweet Ellen,
  Point to the genius bright that crowns her daughter,
And the rare graces that she doth excel in,
  Confessed in floods of praise from every quarter.
The world forgives the wooden nutmeg suction
Because of you, the best Connecticut production.

The succeeding year Miss Chandler passed at Mrs. Willard's Seminary in Troy, N. Y., and a classmate, who in after years became the wife of General Gillespie, thus describes her:

"My acquaintance with Louise Chandler began when she entered Mrs. Willard's Seminary in Troy, where we were both pupils. She was at once very much admired and beloved. Her first book, called 'This, That, and the Other,' had been published just before she came, and we were all very proud of her authorship. She had a lovely face, very fair, with beautiful, wavy, sunny hair, falling on either side the deep blue-gray eyes, with their dark, long lashes. Her voice was clear and sweet, with the most cultivated intonation."

For the school Commencement Miss Chandler was chosen class poet, and produced the regulation poem, neither better nor worse than is usual on such occasions. Six weeks later, August 27, 1855, she married William Upham Moulton, editor and publisher of *The True Flag*, a Boston literary journal to which his bride had been a frequent contributor.

The journalists of the day made many friendly comments upon the marriage of their brother editor. Some of them ran thus:

" The possession of a noble and true heart in the one, and of a gentle and winning nature in the other, are presages of future bliss."

"Mr. Moulton is a writer of much originality of style and great power; an independent thinker, shrewd in conclusions and fearless in expression. Miss Chandler overflows with kindness, geniality, appreciation of the lovely, and the power of description to a remarkable degree."

" . . . Of his choice the world can speak. Her literary attainments have made their public mark, and her kindness of heart has won for her an eminent place in the affections of thousands. Our associate may well be congratulated on his acquisition of a new contributor to his happiness, and pardoned, in view of the richness of his prize, for leaving the fair of our own locality for more distant Connecticut."

One of the girlish pictures of Miss Chandler bears the inscription, in her own writing, "Taken the day I first saw my husband," but unfortunately, the date is not given. In a little sketch Harriet Prescott Spofford remarks that "Louise must have combined studying, writing, and love-making to a rather remarkable degree during her last year at school"; and adds in regard to her marriage:

"She was barely twenty when she married William Upham Moulton, a man of culture and of much personal attraction. Lingering a moment on the church porch in the sunset light, she has been described by one who saw her as a radiant being, in her bridal veil, blooming, blushing, full of life and joy and love. An exquisite skin, the 'rose crushed on ivory,' hazel eyes, with dark lashes and

LOUISE CHANDLER MOULTON, ÆT. 18

Page 34

brows, and a confiding, fearless glance, small white teeth, a delightful smile, cheek and chin having the antique line, all united to make a loveliness which no portrait has successfully rendered, and which tender consideration and grace of manner accented to wonderful charm."

Among her girlish treasures preserved for more than fifty years was a small blank book, on the fly-leaf of which she had written: "Ellen Louise Chandler Moulton, from my husband, Aug. 27, 1855, Elmwood Cottage, Pomfret, Conn."; and underneath in quotation, the lines:

> "Who shall decide? The bridal day, oh, make it
> A day of sacrament and present prayer;
> Though every circumstance conspire to take it
> Out of the common prophecy of care!
> Let not vain merriment and giddy laughter
> Be the last sound in the departing ear,
> For God alone can tell what cometh after —
> What store of sorrow, or what cause to fear."

Mr. Moulton brought his bride to Boston, where she was at once introduced into those literary circles made up of the chief men and women of letters. "Here," said one who remembers her entrance into Boston life, "the bright, quick, impassioned girl

speedily blossomed into the brilliant woman."
In some reminiscences of her own in recalling
this delightful period she said:

"Every one was very good to me — Dr.
Holmes, Longfellow, Whittier — all those on
whose work I had been brought up. And then
the broader religious thought of Boston began
to conquer the Puritanism in which I had been
educated. Whittier was a Quaker, but he
believed most of all in the loving Fatherhood
of God,— the Divine care which would somehow, somewhere, make creation a blessing
to all on whom had been bestowed the unsought gift of life. He told me once how this
conviction first came to him. It was a
touching anecdote of his childhood when his
mother's tenderness to the erring aroused in
him the perception of the goodness of God.
Whittier was a singularly modest man; if
one praised his work he would say, 'Yes, but
there should be a perfection of form, and
what I do is full of faults.' Once, at an
evening party, he was vainly entreated to
recite one of his poems. 'No,' he said, 'but
I wish she would,' pointing to me. I then
read 'The Swan Song of Parson Avery,'
and when I had finished he came across
the room and said, 'Why, thee has really

made me think I 've written a beautiful poem.'

" No words could overpraise the sweet graciousness of Longfellow and Dr. Holmes to me, a new-comer into their world. I knew Ralph Waldo Emerson, also. The very last time I saw him he had just returned from California, and he crossed the Athenæum Library, where we chanced to be, to ask me if I had ever been there myself and had seen the big trees. 'Why,' he said, 'it took thirteen horses to go round one tree, the head of one touching the tail of another — what do you think of that?'

" I remember once, when I was a guest in his house in Concord, his telling me that he had long wanted to make an anthology of the one-poem men. And he went on to speak of the poets who were remembered by only one poem. He never carried out his idea, but I wish some one else might."

It was a rich and stimulating atmosphere into which Mrs. Moulton entered in Boston. The first winter after her marriage Thackeray visited this country and gave in Boston, in January of that year (1856), his lectures on "The Four Georges." In recalling these, Mrs. Moulton afterward said:

brought out anonymously by the Appletons. Again the praise of the reviewers was practically unanimous. A Boston critic wrote: "The authorship is a mystery which perhaps time will unravel, for rumor is ascribing it to lofty names in the world of literature"; and George D. Prentice, in the *Louisville Journal*, in less journalistic phrase, characterized the story as having "numerous points of strange beauty and a strange pathos."

Among the sympathetic friends who at this time enriched Mrs. Moulton's life none was of personality more striking than Mrs. Sarah Helen Whitman, whose connection with Poe was at once so touching and so tragic. "No person ever made on me so purely spiritual an impression," wrote Mrs. Moulton in *The Athenæum* in after years, "as did Mrs. Whitman. One of her friends said of her: 'She is nothing but a soul with a sweet voice.'" Some of the poems signed "Ellen Louise" had attracted the attention of Mrs. Whitman, and a correspondence followed. In a postscript to the first letter written to Mrs. Moulton after her marriage, Mrs. Whitman says:

" You ask my plans. I have none nor ever had. All my life I have been one of those who walk by faith and not by sight. I never

can plan ahead. The first words I ever
learned to speak were caught from hearing
the watchman call out in the middle of the
night, 'All's well.' This has always been
my great article of faith. An angel seems ever
to turn for me at the right time the mystic
pages of the book of life, while I stand wondering and waiting,— that is all."

On the appearance of "Juno Clifford,"
Mrs. Whitman wrote:

Mrs. Whitman to Mrs. Moulton

November 15 [1855].

My Dear Louise: I have read "Juno
Clifford," and my "honest opinion" is that
it is a very fascinating story, eloquently
related. I was surprised at its finished excellence; yet I expected much from you.

I have written a notice for the *Journal* which
will appear in a few days. I will send you a
copy of the paper. I wish I had leisure to
tell you all I think of the book. You have all
the qualities requisite for a successful novelist,
and some very rare ones, as I think. The
grief of the poor Irish girl brought tears to
my eyes,— eyes long accustomed to look
serenely on human sorrows. The character

of Juno is admirably portrayed and you have managed the "heavy tragedy" with admirable skill. I do not, however, like to have Juno tear out her beautiful hair by "handfuls," and I think there is a lavish expenditure of love scenes in the latter part of the book; but all young lovers will freely pardon you for this last offence, and I am not disposed to be hypercritical about the hair.

I can find nothing else to condemn, though I would fain show myself an impartial judge. I wish " Juno " all success, and am ever, with sincere regard,

Your friend,

S. HELEN WHITMAN.

P. S.—I saw the death of Miss Locke in *The Times!* could it have been our Miss Locke? Do you know? I am very busy just now. I have no good pen, and my pencil turns round and round like an inspired Dervish, but utters no sound; so look on my chirography with Christian charity, and love me, nevertheless.

S. H. W.

In other letters from Mrs. Whitman, undated, but evidently written about this time, are these passages:

" I have to-day found time to thank you for your letter and beautiful poem. It is very fine, picturesque, and dramatic. These are, I think, your strong points, but you have touches of pathos. . . . You must not leave off writing stories, nor do I see any necessity of making any selection between the muse of poetry and the muse of romance. I should say, give attendance to both, as the inspiration comes. . . . Dr. Holmes, whom I met at the lectures of Lola Montez, is charmed by her. . . ."

" Mrs. Davis read me Mrs. [R.H.] Stoddard's book ['Two Men'], because you spoke of it so highly. It has, indeed, a strange power, — not one that fascinates me, but which impresses me profoundly and piques my curiosity to know more of the author. I marked some paragraphs which indicated a half-conscious power of imaginative description, which I wish she would exercise more freely. Tell me about her in her personal traits of character. . . . I hope you will not impugn my taste, dear Louise, when I tell you I like your 'two men' better than Mrs. Stoddard's. 'Margaret Holt' is a charming story. Why is it that Mrs. Stoddard so entirely ignores all sweet and noble emotions ? "

Mrs. Moulton's next volume was a collection of the stories which she had contributed to various magazines. It was entitled "My Third Book," and was brought out by the Harpers in 1859. It was greeted as a work which "bears the seal of feminine grace," and which "reveals the beauty of Mrs. Moulton's genius." Of two of the tales a reviewer said, in terms which give with amusing fidelity the tone of the favorable book-notice of the mid-century:

"'No. 101' reminds us of some wondrous statue, her pen has so sculptured the whole story. 'Four Letters from Helen Hamilton' are enough to stir all hearts with their [*sic*] high purpose and the beautiful ideal of womanhood which consecrate [*sic*] them."

Continuing her old habit at school, Mrs. Moulton for many years kept notes of her abundant reading, and the comments and extracts set down in her exquisite handwriting throw a most interesting light on the growth of her thought. She mentions Miss Austen's "Sense and Sensibility" as "interesting, but deficient in earnestness." "Guy Livingston," that old-fashioned apotheosis of brute force, she, like most of the novel-readers of the time, found "fascinating." "The Scarlet

Letter" impresses her profoundly, and she copies many passages; the first volume of "Modern Painters" she reads with the most serious earnestness, and comments at length upon Ruskin's view that public opinion has no claim to be taken as a standard in the judgment of works of art. Although the bride of a few months, and not yet twenty-one, she enters with the enthusiasm of a schoolgirl into the larger opportunities of life opened to her by her marriage. To English literature she gives herself in serious study. She writes copious analyses of the history of different periods, and critical studies of various writers. It was perhaps at this period that she began to respond to the work of the Elizabethan lyricists with a sympathy which marked the kinship which English critics found so evident in her poetic maturity.

The list of books noted in these records during the next ten years is large and varied. Mrs. Gaskell, Bishop Butler, Dr. Martineau, Miss Mulock (Mrs. Craik), Anthony Trollope, and later George Eliot and George Meredith, are among the writers whom she mentions; and from the "Self-Help" of Samuel Smiles in 1860 she makes copious extracts. Her taste was catholic, and her attitude toward literature always one of genuine seriousness.

Mrs. Moulton's memoranda for her own stories are both interesting and suggestive. To see as it were the mind of the creative writer at work is always fascinating, and here, as in the "American Notebooks" of Hawthorne, the reader seems to be assisting in the very laboratory of the imagination. Some of these notes are as follows:

"Have the story written by a man. Have him go all his life worshipping one woman, even from boyhood. He wins her,— she is cold but he is satisfied and believes she will grow to love him. After three years she leaves him. He gives his life to seeking her. At last finds her just as she is attempting to drown herself, and takes her home."

And again:

"Have a wealthy family travelling in Egypt, and a child born to them there who shall bear the name of the country. This child, Egypt Sunderland, seems to be strangely influenced by her name, and develops all the peculiar characteristics of the Egyptian women."

She conceives the outline plots for numerous stories, — among the titles for which are "The Sculptor's Model," "The Unforgiven Sin," "The River Running Fast," "The

Embroidered Handkerchief," "A Wife's Con-
fession," "The Widow's Candle and How
It Went Out." For one projected story her
outline runs:

"Show that there is punishment for our sins
lying in the consequence of them, which no
repentance can avert, or forgiveness condone,
—which must be suffered to the uttermost.
Make it clear that passive goodness is not
enough. We must do something for humanity. That a man who has no moral fibre or
practical wisdom has a claim on us for help.
For energy and good judgment are as much
a gift as are eyes to see and ears to hear.
The very lack of practical wisdom gives the
one so lacking a special claim on our sympathies."

Perhaps no one ever lived more in accord
with this little gospel of human duty than
did Mrs. Moulton, and this fact invests the
note with a peculiar interest.

The fiction of the day was little concerned
with character-drawing or mental analysis,
but was largely occupied with a certain
didactic embodiment of ideals of conduct.
In such fiction a writer of Mrs. Moulton's
genuine sincerity of temperament could not
but show clearly her true attitude toward

the deeper problems of life. The opening of one of her stories, "Margaret Grant," will illustrate this fact.

"The love of life, the love of children, the love of kin — these constrain all of us; but it was another kind of love that constrained Margaret Grant. Curiously enough the first awakening came to her soul from a book written by an unbeliever, a book meant to bring Christianity to the final test of final obedience, and to prove its absurdity, thereby prove that to be a Christian as Christ taught, would overthrow the uses of the world, and uproot the whole system of things. 'Let the uses of the world go, and the system of things take care of itself,' Margaret Grant said when she laid the book down. 'This same religion of Christ is the best thing I know, and I will go where it leads me.' And then she waited for the true Guide, that Holy Spirit which shall be given to every honest soul that seeks — waited for her special work, but not idly, since every day and all the days were the little offices of love that make life sweeter for whatever fellow-pilgrim comes in our way.

"Margaret read to her half-blind grandmother — taught the small boy that ran the

family errands to read — helped her mother
with the housekeeping, all on the lines of
'godly George Herbert,' who wrote:

> Who sweeps a room as for God's laws,
> Makes that and the action fine.

But all the time she felt that these were not
the real work of her life, that work which
was on its way."

With the earnestness of spirit which is
shown in this and which so continually
sounded in her poems, Mrs. Moulton lived
her rich life in the congenial atmosphere
which surrounded her. Mrs. Spofford, writing of Mrs. Moulton from personal memory,
says of her in 1860:

"She was now in her twenty-fifth year, fully
launched upon the literary high-seas, contributing to *Harper's*, the *Galaxy*, and *Scrib-
ner's* as they came into existence, and to
the *Young Folks*, the *Youth's Companion*,
and other periodicals for children. Her life
seemed a fortunate one. She had a charming
home in Boston where she met and entertained
the most pleasant people; her housekeeping
duties were fulfilled to a nicety, and no domes-
tic detail neglected for all her industrious
literary undertakings. A daughter had been

its essence was made up of the charm of noble and sincere friendships, of happy social intercourse, of sympathetic devotion. To this joy of love and friendship, there was in her mind opposed one sorrow — death, and not all the assurances of faith or philosophy could eliminate this dread, this all-pervading fear, that haunted her thoughts. In some way the sadness of death, as a parting, had been stamped on her impressionable nature, and it inevitably colored her outlook and made itself a controlling factor in her character. It took the form, however, of deepening her tenderness for every human relation and widening her charity for all human imperfection. The vision of

> Cold hands folded over a still heart,

touched her as it did Whittier, with the pity of humanity's common sorrow, and with him she could have said that such vision

> Swept all my pride away, and trembling I forgave.

Writing in later years of Stephen Phillips she said :

"Is it not, after all, the comprehension of love that above all else makes a poet immortal ? Who thinks of Petrarch without remembering Laura, of Dante without the vision of Beatrice ? "

" I have said that Phillips is the poet of love and of pity. Many poets have uttered the passionate cries of love; but few, indeed, are those who have seen and expressed the piteous tragedy of life as he has done. He says in ' Marpessa,'

> "The half of music, I have heard men say,
>   Is to have grieved.

And not only has Phillips grieved, but he has felt the grief of other men — listened to the wild, far wail which, one sometimes feels, must turn the very joy of heaven to sorrow."

These words reveal much of her own nature. One critic said aptly:

"She is penetrated with that terrible consciousness of the futility of the life which ends in the grave — that consciousness of personal transitoriness which has haunted and oppressed so many passionate and despairing hearts. She knows that 'there is no name, with whatever emphasis of passionate love repeated, of which the echo is not faint at last.' And against this inevitable doom of humanity she rebels with all the energy of her nature."

In her verse-loving girlhood she had delighted in the facile music and the obvious sentiment of Owen Meredith; his "Aux

It was a period of wonderful literary activity.
Thomas Starr King, who came to Boston in
1845, was a lecturer as well as a preacher
of power and genius. Henry James, the
elder, was publishing from time to time his
philosophic essays, and to Mrs. Moulton,
who was much attracted by his gentle lead-
ings, he gave in generous measure his interest
and encouragement. The *Atlantic Monthly*
was founded in 1857 by Phillips and Sampson,
the enterprising young publishers who, according to Dr. Hale, inaugurated the publishing
business in Boston, and who were the publishers of Mrs. Moulton's first book. With
Lowell, the first editor of the *Atlantic*, Mrs.
Moulton came in contact in the easy intimacy
of the literary atmosphere. She heard with
eager attention the well known lecture of
George William Curtis on "Modern Infi-
delity" in 1860; and in the same year read
with enthusiastic appreciation Hawthorne's
"Marble Faun," from which she made copious
extracts in her notebooks with sympathetic
comments. The artistic and intellectual life
of Boston in those days held much to call out
her keenest interest. Mrs. Kemble gave her
brilliant Shakespearian readings; Patti, a
youthful prima donna, delighted lovers of
opera; Charles Eliot Norton invited friends

to see his new art treasure, a picture by Rossetti; Agassiz was marking an epoch in scientific progress by his lectures. Interested by Professor Agassiz's efforts to found a museum, Mrs. Moulton wrote for the *New York Tribune* a special article on the subject; and this was acknowledged by Mrs. Agassiz.

Mrs. Agassiz to Mrs. Moulton

Thanks for the pleasant and appreciative article about the Agassiz Museum in the *Tribune*. It is a good word spoken in season. It is very charming, and so valuable just now, when the institution is in peril of its life. No doubt it will be of real service in our present difficulties by awakening sympathy and affection in many people. Mr. Agassiz desires his best regards to you.

Yours sincerely,

ELIZABETH CAREY AGASSIZ.

The intellectual and the social were closely blended in the Boston of the sixties and the seventies, and Mrs. Moulton was in the very midst of the most characteristically Bostonian circles. Her journals record how she went to a "great party" given by Mrs. William Claflin, whose husband was afterward governor; to Cambridge to a function given by the

Agassizs; to a reception at Dr. Alger's "to
meet Rose Terry," later known as Rose Terry
Cooke; to a dinner given in honor of Miss
Emily Faithful; to one intellectual gayety after
another. She was one of the attractive figures
at the delightful Sunday evening reunions
given by Mr. and Mrs. Edwin P. Whipple.
She notes in the journal that at a brilliant
reception given by Mrs. John T. Sargent, so
well known as the hostess of the famous
Chestnut Street Radical Club, she had "a
few golden moments" with Emerson, and a
talk with the elder Henry James, with whom
she was a favorite.

In 1870 Mrs. Moulton became the Boston
literary correspondent of the *New York
Tribune*. This work developed under her
care into one of much importance. Boston
publishers sent to her all books of especial
interest, and her comments upon them were
of solid value. She recorded the brilliant
meetings of the Chestnut Street Radical Club,
and the intellectual news in general. These
letters made a distinct success. Extracts
from them were copied all over the United
States, and they came to be looked upon as a
sort of authorized report of what was doing in
the intellectual capital of the country. They
were given up only when the desire for for-

eign travel drew Mrs. Moulton so much
abroad that she could no longer keep as
closely in touch with current events as is
necessary for a press correspondent.

The Radical Club at that time was famed
throughout the entire country, and it was regarded as the very inner temple wherein the
gods forged their thunderbolts. Only those
who bore the sacramental sign were supposed
to pass its portals. Mrs. Moulton's accounts
of these meetings were vivid and significant.
As, for instance, the following:

"The brightest sun of the season shone, and
the balmiest airs prevailed, on the 21st of
December, in honor of the meeting of the
Radical Club under the hospitable roof of
Mr. and Mrs. John T. Sargent in Chestnut
street. Mrs. Howe was the essayist, and there
was a brilliant gathering to hear her. David
Wasson was there, and John Weiss, and
Colonel Higginson, and Alcott, hoary embodiment of cool, clear thought. Mr. Linton, the
celebrated engraver, John Dwight of the
Musical Journal, Mrs. Severance, the beloved president of the New England Woman's
Club, bonny Kate Field of the honest eyes and
the piquant pen, Mrs. Cheney, Miss Peabody,
and many others, distinguished in letters or art.

"To this goodly company Mrs. Howe read a brilliant essay on the subject of Polarity. She commenced by speaking of polarity as applied to matter, in a manner not too abstruse for the *savants* who surrounded her, though it was too philosophical and scholarly to receive the injustice of being reported. The progress of polarity she found to give us the division of sex; and Sex was the subject on which she intended to write when she commenced the essay; but she found it, like all fundamental facts in nature, to be an idea with a history. In the pursuit of this history she encountered the master agency of Polarity, and found herself obliged to make that the primary idea, and consider sex as derived from it."

Another letter, describing a meeting a few weeks later, gives a glimpse at some of the women who frequented the club:

"There was Mrs. Severance, reminding one so much of an Indian summer day, so calm and peaceful is the sweet face that looks out at you from its framing of fair waving hair. Not far away was Julia Ward Howe, who some way or other makes you think of the old fairy story of the girl who never opened her mouth but there fell down before her pearls and diamonds. That story is n't a fairy story, not a bit of it. It is real, genuine truth, and Mrs. Howe is the girl grown up, and pearls of poetic fancy and diamonds of sparkling wit are the precious stones which fall from her lips. Lucy Stone was there, an attentive listener, looking the very picture of retiring womanliness in her Quaker-like simplicity of dress, and her pleasant face lighted with interest and animation. Sitting by a table, busy with notebook and pencil, was Miss Peabody, the Secretary of the Club. She has a sparkling, animated face, brimming over with kindness and good-will; she wins one strangely — you can't help being drawn to her. There's a world of fun in the black eyes, and you feel sure she would appreciate the ridiculous sides of living as keenly as any one ever could."

In still another letter are these thumb-nail sketches of persons well-known:

"As we drew near Chestnut street we saw a goodly number of pilgrims. . . . Nora Perry, with the golden hair, had journeyed up from Providence with a gull's feather in her hat and a glint of mischief in her glance; Celia Thaxter, whom the Atlantic naturally delights to honor, since from Atlantic surges she caught the rhythm of her life, sat intent; Mr. Alcott beamed approval; Professor Goodwin

had come from Harvard; David A. Wasson
had left his bonded ware-house a prey to
smugglers; Rev. Dr. Bartol, who seems always to dwell on the Mount of Vision; and
Mr. Sanborn, who had sheathed his glittering
lance, sat near; Mrs. Howe, taking a little
vacation from her labors for women, listened
serenely; Miss Peabody had a good word to
say for Aspasia; and Mrs. Cheney quoted
Walter Savage Landor's opinion of her."

A racy letter tells of the meeting when the
Club discovered Darwin; another deals with
the day when Mrs. Howe discoursed of "Moral
Trigonometry"; and yet another of an occasion when the Rev. Samuel Longfellow was
essayist, and all the pretty women had new
bonnets. This allusion reminds one of a bit
of witty verse when "Sherwood Bonner" (Mrs.
McDowell) served up the Radical Club in a
parody of Poe's "Raven," and described Mrs.
Moulton as,

"A matron made for kisses, in the loveliest of dresses."

The "Twelve Apostles of Heresy," as the
transcendental   thinkers   were   irreverently
termed by the wits of the press, were about
this time contributing to the enlightenment of
the public by a series of Sunday afternoon

lectures. These lectures were held to represent the most advanced thought of the day, and were delivered by such speakers as the Rev. O. B. Frothingham, Mary Grew (Whittier's friend and a woman of equally cultivated mind and lovely character), the Rev. John Weiss, Mrs. Julia Ward Howe, T. W. Higginson, and Mrs. Ednah D. Cheney. In one letter Mrs. Moulton writes thus:

" As the coffin of Mahomet was suspended between heaven and earth, so is Mr. Wasson, who spoke last Sunday at Horticultural Hall, popularly supposed to be suspended between the heaven of Mr. Channing's serene faith and the depths of Mr. Abbot's audacious heresy. But if any one should infer from this statement that Mr. Wasson is a gentle medium, a man without boldness of speculation, or originality of thought, he would find he had never in his life made so signal a mistake. Few men in America think so deeply as David A. Wasson, and fewer still have so many of the materials for thought at their command. He has a presence of power, and is a handsome man, though prematurely gray, with an expansive forehead, where strong thoughts and calm judgment sit enthroned, and with eyes beneath it which see very far indeed. His features are clearly cut, and he looks as if he felt, and felt passionately, every word he utters, as he stands before an audience, his subject well in hand, and with always twice as much to say as his hour will give space for, forced, therefore, against his will, to choose and condense from his thronging thoughts. He spoke, in the Sunday afternoon course, on 'Jesus, Christianity, and Modern Radicalism.'"

John Weiss, the biographer of Theodore Parker, discoursed on one occasion on "The Heaven of Homer," and Mrs. Moulton commented:

"Not the author of 'Gates Ajar,' listening in her pleasant dreams to heavenly pianos, ever drew half so near to the celestial regions, or looked into them with half so disillusionized gaze as the Grecian thought of the time of Homer."

Of Mary Grew Mrs. Moulton gave this pen-picture:

"We saw a woman not young, save with the youth of the immortals; not beautiful, save with the beauty of the spirit; but sweet and gentle, with a placid, earnest face. Her own faith is so assured that she appeals fearlessly to the faith of others; her nature so religious that her religion seems a fact and not a question."

Another Boston institution of which Mrs. Moulton wrote in her *Tribune* letters was the New England Woman's Club. "Here," she declared, "Mrs. Howe reads essays and poems in advance of their publication; Abby May's wit flashes keen; Mrs. Cheney gives lovely talks on art; and Kate Field, with the voice which is music, reads her first lecture." She records how Emerson sends to the club-tea a poem; how Whittier is sometimes a guest; how Miss Alcott tells an inimitable story; and how on May 23, 1870, was celebrated the birthday of Margaret Fuller, who for a quarter of a century had been beyond the count of space and time. On this occasion the Rev. James Freeman Clarke presided, and among the papers was a poem by Mrs. Howe of which Mrs. Moulton quotes the closing stanza:

> Fate dropt our Margaret
> Within the bitter sea,
> A pearl in golden splendor set
> For spirit majesty.

It was in connection with a meeting of the Woman's Club that a guest invited from New York wrote for a journal of that city an account of the gathering in which is this description:

"There too was Mrs. Louise Chandler Moulton, looking for all the world like one of

5

Longfellow commended her perfection of form and the lyric spontaneity of her verse and Whittier urged her to collect and publish her poems in a volume.

Various letters of interest during these years from and to Mrs. Moulton are as follows:

Mr. Whittier to Mrs. Moulton

AMESBURY, 3d, 8th month, 1870.

DEAR MRS. MOULTON: I am greatly disappointed in not meeting the benediction of thy face when I called last month; but I shall seek it again sometime. It just occurs to me that I may yet have the pleasure of seeing thee under my roof at Amesbury. We have so many friends in common that I feel as if I knew thee through them.

How much I thank thee for thy kind note. It reaches me at a time when its generous appreciation is very welcome and grateful.

Believe me very truly thy friend,

JOHN G. WHITTIER.

William Winter to Mrs. Moulton

STATEN ISLAND, N. Y.
November 8, 1875.

DEAR MRS. MOULTON: I accept with pleasure and gratitude your very kind and sympathetic letter, — seeing beneath its delicate and cordial words the sincere heart of a comrade in literature, and the regard of a nature kindred with my own. I wish I could think that your praise is deserved. It has often seemed to me of late that there is no cheer in my newspaper work. . . . I am aware, however, that the sympathy of a bright mind and a tender heart and the approval of a delicate taste are not won without some sort of merit, and so I venture to find in your most genial and spontaneous letter a ray of encouragement. You will scarcely know how grateful this is to me at this time. I thank you and I shall not forget that you were thoughtful and delicately kind.

To-day I have received a copy of Stedman's poems, which I want to read again with great care. A man who has missed poetic fame himself may find great satisfaction in the success of his friend, and I do feel exceedingly glad in the recognition that has come to Stedman. Your article on the book in the *Tribune* was excellent.

Faithfully yours,

WILLIAM WINTER.

treated me far better than I had any reason to expect; and I have been blessed with dear friends, whose love is about me like an atmosphere.

I have read the little poem enclosed in thy letter with a feeling of tenderest sympathy. God help us! The loneliness of life, under even the best circumstances, becomes at times appalling to contemplate. We are all fearfully alone; no one human soul can fully know another, and an infinite sigh for sympathy is perpetually going up from the heart of humanity. But doubtless this very longing is the pledge and prophecy and guarantee of an immortal destination. Perfect content is stagnation and ultimate death.

Why does thee not publish thy poems? Everywhere I meet people who have been deeply moved by them.

Thy letter dates from Pomfret, and I direct there to thee. I was in that place once so long ago that thee must have been a mere child. I rode over its rocky hills, bare in the chill December, with the late William H. Burleigh. I think it must be charming in summer and autumn. But something in thy poems and in thy letter leads me to infer that thy sojourn there has not been a happy one. Of course I do not speak of unalloyed happiness, for that can only come of entire exemption from sin and weakness. A passage which I have been reading this morning from Thomas à Kempis has so spoken to my heart that I venture to transcribe it:

"What thou canst not amend in thyself or others, bear with patience until God ordaineth otherwise. When comfort is taken away do not presently despair. Stand with an even mind, resigned to the will of God, whatever may befall; for after winter cometh the summer, after the dark night the day shineth, and after the storm cometh a great calm."

Believe me always gratefully thy friend,

JOHN G. WHITTIER.

Religious questions, with which Mrs. Moulton was always deeply concerned, come often into her letters. To Mr. Stedman she writes:

"I have been curiously interested of late about a band of 'Sanctificationists,' who believe Christ meant it when He said, He can save from all sin. So they reason that, trusting in His own words, they can be saved from sin now and here. There is about them a peace and serenity, a sweetness and light, a joy in believing, that is unmistakable. They do live happier lives than others. I cannot believe, somehow, in this 'cleansing blood,' yet, seeing these people, I feel that I lose a great deal by not believing in it. Oh, if one only knew the truth! Reason rejects, it seems to me, the orthodox dogmas, but what is one to do with the argument of holier lives?"

Unconsciously Mrs. Moulton was echoing Emerson's lines,

> Nor knowest thou what argument
> Thy life to thy neighbor's creed has lent.

To the late sixties belongs a little incident which illustrates well Mrs. Moulton's attitude toward society. She was fond of social life, but it was in her interest always secondary to the intellectual. During a visit to New York, she was one evening just dressed for a festivity which she was to attend with her hostess, when the card of Horace Greeley was brought to her. She went down at once, and Mr. Greeley, who probably would not have noted any difference between a ball-gown and a negligé did not in the least appreciate that she was evidently dressed for a social function. When her hostess came to call her, Mrs. Moulton signalled that she was to be left, and passed the evening in conversation so interesting and so animated that Mr. Greeley remained until an unusually late hour. Just as he was leaving he seemed to become dimly conscious that her costume was especially elaborate, and he inquired innocently:

"But were you not going somewhere to-night?"

"One does not go 'somewhere,'" she returned, "at the expense of missing a conversation with Mr. Greeley."

In 1873 Mrs. Moulton published a volume for young folk entitled "Bed-Time Stories." It was issued by Roberts Brothers, who from this time until the dissolution of the firm in 1898, after the death of Mr. Niles, remained her publishers. The success of the book was immediate, and so great that the title was repeated in "More Bed-Time Stories," brought out in the year following. The first volume was dedicated to her daughter in these graceful lines:

It is you that I see, my darling,
    On every page of this book,
With your flowing golden tresses,
    And your wistful, wondering look,

As you used to linger and listen
    To the "Bed-time Stories" I told,
Till the sunset glory faded,
    And your hair was the only gold.

Will another as kindly critic
  So patiently hear them through?
Will the many children care for
  The tales that I told to you?

You smile, sweetheart, at my question;
  For answer your blue eyes shine:
"We will please the rest if it may be,
  But the tales are — yours and mine."

Of the second series of "Bed-Time Stories"
George H. Ripley wrote in the *Tribune:*

"The entire absence of all the visible signs
of art in the composition of these delightful
stories betrays a rare degree of artistic culture
which knows how to conceal itself, or a singular natural bent to graceful and picturesque
expression. Perhaps both of these conditions
best explain the secret of their felicitous con-
struction, and their fidelity to nature. The
best fruits of sweet womanly wisdom she
deems not too good for the entertainment of
the young souls with whom she cherishes
such a cordial sympathy, and whom she so
graciously attracts by the silvery music of
her song, which lacks no quality of poetry
but the external form. . . . They incul-
cate no high-flown moral, but inspire the
noblest sentiments. There is no preaching
in their appeals, but they offer a perpetual

incentive to all that is lovely and good in character."

An equal success attended the collection of stories for older readers which Mrs. Moulton brought out a year later under the title, "Some Women's Hearts." This contained all the stories written since the appearance of "My Third Book" which she thought worthy of preservation, and may be said to represent her best in this order of fiction. Professor Moses Coit Tyler said of them: "Mrs. Moulton has the incommunicable tact of the story-teller"; commented on their freedom from all padding, and commended their complete unity. The instinct for literary form which was so strikingly conspicuous in her verse showed itself in these stories by the excellence of arrangement and proportion, the sincerity and earnestness which made the tales vital. She had by this time outgrown the rather sentimental fashions of the gift-book period of American letters, and her conscientious and careful criticism of the work of others had resulted in a power of self-criticism which was admirable in its results. "My best reward," she said in after years, "has been the friendships that my slight work has won for me"; but by the time she was forty she had won a place in American letters such as had been held by only two or three other women, and before her was the reputation which she was to win abroad, such as no woman of her country had ever attained before.

CHAPTER IV

1876–1880

For I dipt into the future, far as human eye could see,
Saw the Vision of the world, and all the wonder that would be.
TENNYSON.

The winds to music strange were set;
The sunsets glowed with sudden flame. — L. C. M.

MRS. MOULTON made her first visit to Europe in January, 1876. She remained abroad for nearly two years. From that date until the summer of 1907, inclusive, she passed every summer but two on the other side of the Atlantic. London became her second home. Her circle of friends, not only in England but on the Continent, became very wide. Her poems were published in England, and she was accorded in London society a place of distinction such as had not before been given to any American woman of letters. She enjoyed her social opportunities; but she prized most the number of sincere and interesting friendships which resulted from them. It is not difficult to understand how her charm and kindliness won those she met, or how her friendliness and sympathy endeared her to all who came to know her well.

Mrs. Moulton's first glimpse of London was simply what could be had in a brief pause on her way to Paris. She was, however, present in the House of Lords when the Queen opened Parliament in person for the first time after the death of the Prince Consort. She stayed but a few days in Paris, and then hastened on to Rome. Mrs. Harriet Prescott Spofford thus describes this first visit to the Immortal City:

"Paris over, came Rome, and twelve weeks of raptures and ruins, of churches and galleries, old palaces and almond-trees in flower, the light upon the Alban Hills, the kindly, gracious Roman society, all like a dream from which might come awaking. Certainly no one was ever made to feel the ancient spell, or to enjoy its beauty more than this sensitive, sympathetic, and impressible spirit. Stiff Protestant as she is, she was touched to tears by the benignant old pope's blessing; and she abandoned herself to the carnival, as much a child as 'the noblest Roman of them all.'"

Mrs. Moulton entered into the artistic life
of Rome with characteristic ardor. She knew
many artists, and became an especial friend
of Story's, a visitor at his studio, and an
admirer of his sculpture.

"I had greatly liked many of his poems,"
she said later, "and I was curious to see if his
poems in marble equalled them. I was more
than charmed with his work; and I suppose
I said something which revealed my enthusiasm, for I remember the smile — half of
pleasure, half of amusement — with which
he looked at me. He said: 'You don't
seem to feel quite as an old friend of mine
from Boston felt, when he went through my
studio, and, at least, I showed him the best
I had. We are all vain, you know; and I
suppose I expected a little praise, but my
legal friend shook his head. "Ah, William,"
he said, "you might have been a great lawyer
like your father; you had it in you; but you
chose to stay on here and pinch mud"!'
Another American sculptor whom Rome delighted to honor is Mr. Richard S. Greenough,
whose 'Circe' has more fascination for me
than almost anything else in modern art;
but my acquaintance with him came later. I
had a letter of introduction to William and

6

moment; then he called out to some one
standing near, 'Look here, Mrs. Moulton
wants to know which one of us is Browning.
C'est moi!' he added with a gay gesture;
and this is how my friendship with the author
of 'Pippa Passes' began."

This introduction may be said to have
"placed" Mrs. Moulton in English literary
society, and there was hardly a person of
intellectual distinction in London whom she
did not meet. She came to know the Rossettis,
William Sharp, Theodore Watts (later known
as Watts-Dunton), Herbert E. Clarke, Mrs.
W. K. Clifford, A. Mary F. Robinson (afterward Mme. Darmesteter), Olive Schreiner,
Lewis Morris, William Bell Scott, the Hon.
Roden Noel, Iza Duffus Hardy, Aubrey de
Vere, the Marstons, father and son, and in
short almost every writer worth knowing.
She came, indeed, to belong almost as completely to the London literary world as to
that of America.

Philip Bourke Marston, the blind poet,
whose friend and biographer she in time became, she first met on the first day of July of
this year. She has recorded the meeting:

" It was just six weeks before his twenty-
sixth birthday. He was tall, slight, and, in

spite of his blindness, graceful. He seemed
to me young-looking even for his twenty-six
years. He had a noble and beautiful forehead. His brown eyes were perfect in shape,
and even in color, save for a dimness like a
white mist that obscured the pupil, but which
you perceived only when you were quite near
to him. His hair and beard were dark
brown, with warm glints of chestnut; and the
color came and went in his cheeks as in those
of a sensitive girl. His face was singularly
refined, but his lips were full and pleasure-
loving, and suggested dumbly how cruel must
be the limitations of blindness to a nature hun-
gry for love and for beauty. I had been greatly
interested, before seeing him, in his poems,
and to meet him was a memorable delight.

" He and the sister, who was his inseparable
companion, soon became my close friends,
and with them both this friendship lasted
till the end."

The poetry of Swinburne had for her a
fascination from the first, and she was attracted
also by the personality of the poet. Writing
an article upon a new volume of his, she
submitted the copy to him before publishing
it in the *Athenæum*. His acknowledgment
was as follows:

up their swift march and counter-march
All this time Dr. Marston talked as we saun
tered on, and talked superbly. I think th
electricity in the air inspired him. He talke
of the soul's destiny, of immortality, an
expressed, with matchless eloquence, tha
strong-winged faith which bears him o
toward that end that will be, he feels sure
the new life's beginning. From time to tim
he interrupted himself to point out some
thing that we might not else have seen,—
some wonderful phantom of moonlight, som
cottage-lamp shining at the end of a long lane
some Rembrandt contrast of light and shade

"We walked far, but I knew no weariness
I could have walked on forever watchin
that strange and fitful sky, and listening t
such talk as I have seldom heard. Here i
an affluent poet, who affords to scatter hi
riches broadcast, and does not save them a
for his printed pages. We went home a
last and sat for a while in Dr. Marston'
house, and then Philip and Cecily and I wen
down to the long terrace overlooking the sea
and sat for an hour or more to watch th
moonlight on the breaking waves. How happ
we were, that little while! We talked of th
fitful clouds, the wild, hurrying sea, the white
sweet moon. Then something brought bac

to me visions of the white statues at Rome, and I tried to show them how fair these old gods stood in my memory. Ah! shall I ever forget this so lovely night? The strange, changeful, wind-swept sky, the waves swollen with the passion of yesterday's storm, marching in like a strong army upon the shore and overwhelming it. Behind us the casino, with its many lights, and down there between the moonlight and the sea, we three who did not know each other three months ago but hold each other so closely now.

"Nothing can ever take from me the fitful splendor, the wild rhythm, the divine mystery of this happy night. I can always close my eyes and see again sea and sky and dear faces; hear again the waves break on this wild coast of Normandy, with the passion of their immortal pain and longing."

This stay in Etretat was further commemorated in her poem of that title. Dr. Marston, too, felt the spell of the place and company, and addressed to her this sonnet:

THE EMBALMING OF A DAY.

TUESDAY: SEPTEMBER 11: 1877. To LOUISE.

Day hath Lived! So let him fall asleep.
A Day is Dead — Days are not born again.
Only his Spirit shall for Us remain

Who found Him dear: His Hours in Balm to steep
Of all sweet Thoughts that may in Freshness keep
    The beauty of a Day forever slain —
    Of Wishes, for the bitter Herbs of Pain:
Of Looks that meet and smile, though Hearts may weep.
So shall our Night to come not wholly prove
    An Egypt's Feast, where bids the Silent Guest
"In Joy remember Death." — "Remember Love
    In Death," thy dead Day breathes from Breast to Breast.
Embalm Him thus, Heart's Love, that he may lie
Untombed and unforgotten, though he die.

The succeeding winter Mrs. Moulton passed
in Paris. Here as in London she met many
of the most interesting people of the day.
With Stéphane Mallarmé especially she formed
a close friendship, and through him she came
to know the chief men of the group called at
that time the *"Décadents"* of which he was
the leader. Mallarmé was at this time professor of English in a French college, and
his use of that language afforded Mrs. Moulton some amusement. "He always addressed
me in the third person," she related, "and he
made three syllables of 'themselves.' He
spoke of useless things as 'unuseful.' He was,
however, a great comfort and pleasure to me,
and I saw a great deal of him and of his wife
that winter. I used to dine with them at their
famous Tuesdays, and meet the adoring
throng that came in after dinner. Often he
and Madame Mallarmé would saunter with

me about the streets of Paris. It was then
that I first made acquaintance with the
French dolls, — those wonderful creations
which can bow and courtesy and speak, and
are so much better than humans that they always do the thing they should. Whenever
we came to a window where one of these
lovely creatures awaited us, I used to insist
upon stopping to make her dollship's acquaintance, until I fear the Mallarmés really
believed that these dolls were the most allur-
ing things in life to me. But the winter, —
crowded for me with the deepest interests and
delights in meeting the noted men of letters
and many of the greatest artists, and of studying that new movement in art, Impressionism,
which was destined to be so revolutionary in
its influence, — at last this wonderful winter
came to an end, and I was about to cross the
Channel once more. Full of kindly regrets
came Monsieur and Madame Mallarmé to pay
me a parting call. 'We have wishéd,' began the poet, mustering his best English in
compliment to the occasion, 'Madame and I
have wishéd to make to Madame Moulton a
souvenir for the good-bye, and we have
thought much, we have consideréd the pref-
erence beautiful of Madame, so refinéd; and
we do reflect that as Madame is pleaséd to

so graciously the dolls of Paris like, we have wishéd to a doll present her. Will Madame do us the pleasure great to come out and choose with us a doll, *très jolie*, that may have the pleasure to please her?'''

It would be a pleasure to record that Mrs. Moulton accepted the gift. The doll presented by the leader of the Symbolists would have been not only historic, but it might have been regarded as signifying in the language of symbolism things unutterable; but she could only say: "Oh, no; please. I should be laughed at. Please let it be something else." And the guests retired pensive, to return next day with a handsome Japanese cabinet as their offering. "And I have pined ever since," Mrs. Moulton added smilingly, when she told the story, "for the Mallarmé doll that might have been mine."

In 1877 the Macmillans brought out Mrs. Moulton's first volume of poems under the title "Swallow Flights," the name being taken from Tennyson's well known lines:

> Short swallow-flights of song, that dip
> Their wings in tears, and skim away.

The American edition, which followed soon after from the house of Roberts Brothers, was entitled simply "Poems." The success of the book was a surprise to the author. Professor William Minto wrote in the *Examiner*:

"We do not, indeed, know where to find, among the works of English poetesses, the same self-controlled fulness of expression with the same depth and tenderness of simple feeling. . . . 'One Dread' might have been penned by Sir Philip Sidney."

The *Athenæum*, always chary of over-praise, declared:

"It is not too much to say of these poems that they exhibit delicate and rare beauty, marked originality, and perfection of style. What is still better, they impress us with a sense of subtle and vivid imagination, and that spontaneous feeling which is the essence of lyrical poetry. . . . A poem called 'The House of Death' is a fine example of the writer's best style. It paints briefly, but with ghostly fidelity, the doomed house, which stands blind and voiceless amid the light and laughter of summer. The lines which we print in italics show a depth of suggestion and a power of epithet which it would be difficult to surpass.

"THE HOUSE OF DEATH

" Not a hand has lifted the latchet,
    Since she went out of the door, —
No footsteps shall cross the threshold,
    Since she can come in no more.

"There is rust upon locks and hinges,
    And mould and blight on the walls,
And silence faints in the chambers,
    And darkness waits in the halls, —

" Waits, as all things have waited,
    Since she went, that day of spring,
Borne in her pallid splendour,
    To dwell in the Court of the King;

" With lilies on brow and bosom,
    With robes of silken sheen,
And her wonderful frozen beauty
    The lilies and silk between.

.   .   .   .

" *The birds make insolent music*
    Where the sunshine riots outside;
And the winds are merry and wanton,
    With the summer's pomp and pride.

" But into this desolate mansion,
    Where Love has closed the door,
Nor sunshine nor summer shall enter,
    Since she can come in no more."

Philip Bourke Marston wrote a long review of the volume in *The Academy*, London,
in the course of which he admirably sum-

marized the merits of the work when he
said:

"The distinguishing qualities of these poems
are extreme directness and concentration
of utterance, unvarying harmony between
thought and expression, and a happy freedom from that costly elaboration of style so
much in vogue. . . . Yet, while thus free
from elaboration, Mrs. Moulton's style dis-
plays rare felicity of epithet. . . . The poeti-
cal faculty of the writer is in no way more
strongly evinced than by the subtlety and
suggestiveness of her ideas."

The reviewers of note on both sides of the
Atlantic were unanimous in their praise. In
a time of æsthetic imitation she came as an
absolutely natural singer. She gave the
effect of the sudden note of a thrush heard
through a chorus of mocking-birds and pip-
ing bullfinches. She was able to put herself
into her work and yet to keep her poetry free
from self-consciousness; and to be at once
spontaneous and impassioned is given to few
writers of verse. When such a power belongs
to an author the verse becomes poetry.

Mrs. Moulton had already come to regard
Robert Browning as, in her own phrase,
"king of contemporary poets." She sent to

him a copy of "Swallow Flights," with a timid, graceful note asking for his generosity. In his acknowledgment he said:

Mr. Browning to Mrs. Moulton

19 WARWICK CRESCENT, W.
February 24, '78.

MY DEAR MRS. MOULTON: Thank you for the copy of the poems. They need no generosity. . . . I close it only when needs I must at page the last, with music in my ears and flowers before my eyes, and not without thoughts across the brain. Pray continue your "flights," and be assured of the sympathetic observation of

Yours truly,
ROBERT BROWNING.

In acknowledgment of a copy of "In the Garden of Dreams" William Winter wrote:

Mr. Winter to Mrs. Moulton

"It is a beautiful book, Louise, and the spirit of it is tender, dreamlike and sorrowful. . . . The pathos of it affects me strongly. Life appeals more strongly to you than the pageantry. There is more fancy in your poems and more alacrity and variety of thought, but the quality that impresses me is feeling. I

19. Warwick Crescent, W

Feb 24. '78.

Dear Mrs Moulton,

Thank you very much for the
gift of your Poems: they need no "gene=
=rosity," and get more justice when I say
I, having begun the book = somewhat
"more than five minutes" ago, — I close it only
as needs I must — at page the last, with
music in my ears and flowers before my
eyes, — not without thoughts across the brain.
May continue your flights, and be assured
of the sympathetic observance of
Yours Truly
Robert Browning.

am not a critic, but somehow I must feel that
I know a good thing when I see it, and I am
sure that no one but a true artist in poetry
could have written those stanzas called 'Now
and Then.'   The music has been running in
my mind for days and days,

"And had you loved me then, my dear.

I think you are very kind to remember me
and to send such a lovely offering to me at
Christmas.   God bless you! and may this
new year be happy for you, and the harbinger
of many happier years to follow."

Some years later the Scotch critic, Professor Meiklejohn, sent to Mrs. Moulton a
series of comments which he had made while
reading "Swallow Flights," "in the intervals
of that fearful kind of business called Ex-
amination;" and some of these may be
quoted before the book is passed for other
matters.

"The word 'waiting' in the line

' White moons made beautiful the waiting night,'

is full of emotional and imaginative memory.
"In 'A Painted Fan' the line

'The soft, south wind of memory blows,'

7

simple in phraseology. It gave one a sense of intimacy with God, in which was no irreverence. The sermon commenced at 12 m., and lasted three-quarters of an hour. I thought John Bunyan might have preached just such a discourse."

To her great regret she missed meeting Tennyson. Long afterward she wrote:

"I never met Tennyson, but I just lost him by an accident. I shall never get over the regret of it. I had been invited to various places where he was expected as a guest; but you know how elusive he was, even his best friends could get at him but rarely. One day I had gone out for some idiotic shopping — shopping is always idiotic to me — and when I came back at late dinner time Lord Houghton met me with the question, 'Where have you been? I've been sending messengers all over the city for you. I got hold of Tennyson, and he waited for half an hour to see you.' The fates were never kind enough to bring me within the poet's range again."

On the death of Mrs. Sarah Helen Whitman in 1878, Mrs. Moulton wrote of her in the London *Athenæum*. The admiration of Poe which exists in England, the romance of his

relations with the "Helen" of his most beautiful poem, made the article especially timely;
and from her acquaintance and her warm
friendship for Mrs. Whitman, Mrs. Moulton
was able to speak with authority. Her description of the personality of Mrs. Whitman
is noteworthy:

" There was a singular attraction in the personal presence of this woman. The rooms
where she lived habitually were full of her.
They were dim, shadowy rooms, rich in tone,
crowded with objects of interest, packed with
the memorials of a lifetime of friendships;
but she herself was always more interesting
than her surroundings. When she died, her
soft brown hair was scarcely touched with
gray. Her voice retained to the last its music,
vibrating at seventy-five with the sympathetic
cadences of her youth. She was singularly
shy. I remember that when I persuaded her
to repeat to me one of her poems, she always
insisted on going behind me. She could not
bring herself to confront eye and ear at the
same time."

The letters of Mrs. Whitman to Mrs. Moulton have been published in the biography of
the former, but the following is so unusual —
"the lady's gentle vexation at having been

Derbyshire, one mile from Haddon Hall. Go there. And do not forget to write to me.

Truly yours,

HENRY W. LONGFELLOW.

In October, 1879, Mr. Chandler died, and Mrs. Moulton's grief was sincere and deep. It was the beginning of the breaking of the relations which had been closest in her life. Her love for her father had been always tender and fine, and both her journal and her letters show how much she felt the loss.

She was in America at the time of her father's death, and in correspondence with many of the friends she had made abroad. Among her Christmas gifts this year came a sonnet from Dr. Westland Marston.

To L. C. M.

Take thou, as symbol of thyself, this rose
Which blooms in our world's winter.
  Dank and prone
Lie rose-stems now, by sleety gales o'erthrown,
But still thy flower in hall and chamber glows,
Fed, like thee, not by airs the garden knows,
  But by a subtler climate. Thus the zone
  Of Summer binds the seasons, one to one,
And links the beam which dawns with that which goes.

Hail, Human Rose! — With heavenly fires enshrined,
  Still cheat worn hearts anew in fond surprise
  To faith in Youth's dear, dissipated skies;

LUCIUS LEMUEL CHANDLER, MRS. MOULTON'S FATHER

Page 104

Soul-flower, still shed thine influence!
   Sun nor wind
  Control not thee; thy life thy charm supplies
And makes the beauty which it does not find.

W. M.

Christmas Eve.

CHAPTER V

1880-1890

The busy shuttle comes and goes
  Across the rhymes, and deftly weaves
  A tissue out of autumn leaves,
With here a thistle, there a rose.

With art and patience thus is made
  The poet's perfect Cloth of Gold;
  When woven so, nor earth nor mould
Nor time can make its colors fade. — T. B. ALDRICH.

And others came. — Desires and Adorations;
  Winged Persuasions and veiled Destinies;
Splendors and Glooms and glimmering Incantations
  Of hopes and fears and twilight fantasies. — SHELLEY.

I see the Gleaming Gates and toward them press. — L. C. M.

MR. and Mrs. Moulton when they first
set up their household gods established themselves on Beacon Hill. A
few years later, however, a new part of the
city was developed at the South End, and
popular favor turned in that direction. The
broad streets and squares with trees and
turf were quiet and English-looking, and

although fickle fashion has in later years forsaken the region, it remains singularly attractive. Here Mr. Moulton became the owner of a house, and for the remainder of their lives he and his wife made this their home.

The dwelling was a four-story brick house, the front windows looking out upon the greenery of a little park in the centre of the square. At one end of the place was a stone church, defined against the sky and especially lovely with the red of sunset behind it; and an old-world atmosphere of retirement and leisure always pervaded the region. In Rutland Square, No. 28 came to be well known to every Bostonian and to whomever among visitors was interested in things literary. It was the most cosmopolitan centre of social life in the city; and to it famous visitors to this country were almost sure to find their way. For thirty years Mrs. Moulton's weekly receptions through the winter were notable.

The drawing-room and library where groups of charming and famous people assembled were such as to remain pictured in the memory of the visitor. They were fairly furnished, so to speak, with the tributes of friends. There were water-colors from Rollin Tilton of Rome; a vigorous sketch of a famous

group of trees at Bordighera by Charles Caryl
Coleman; a number of signed photographs
from Vedder; sketches in clay from Greenough, Ezekiel, and Robert Barrett Browning; a group of water-colors, illustrating Mrs.
Moulton's poem, "Come Back, Dear Days,"
by Winthrop Pierce, — one of these showing
a brilliant sunrise, while underneath was the
line,

"The morning skies were all aflame;"

and another, revealing a group of shadow-
faces, illustrated the line,

"I see your gentle ghosts arise."

There were signed photographs of Robert
Barrett Browning's "Dryope," a gift from
the artist; a painting of singular beauty
from the artist, Signor Vertunni, of Rome;
and from William Ordway Partridge three
sculptures,— the figure of a child in Carrara
marble, a head tinted like old ivory, and a
portrait bust of Edward Everett Hale, a
speaking likeness. There was that wonderful
drawing by Vedder, "The Cup of Death"
(from the Rubaiyat), which the artist had
given to Mrs. Moulton in memory of her
sonnet on the theme, the opening lines of
which are:

The Library in Mrs. Moulton's Boston Home, 28 Rutland Square

Page 109

She bends her lovely head to taste thy draught,
O thou stern "Angel of the Darker Cup,"
With thee to-night in the dim shades to sup,
Where all they be who from that cup have quaffed.

And among the rare books was a copy of Stéphane Mallarmé's translation of Poe's "Raven," with illustrations by Manet, the work being the combined gift to Mrs. Moulton of the poet-translator and the artist.

Many were the rare books in autograph copies given to Mrs. Moulton by her friends abroad — copies presented by Lord Houghton, George Eliot, Tennyson, Jean Ingelow, Christina Rossetti, Oswald Crawfurd, George Meredith, Robert Louis Stevenson, Arthur O'Shaughnessy, and several, too, which were dedicated to her,— the "Wind Voices" of Philip Bourke Marston, inscribed: "To Louise Chandler Moulton, true poet and true friend," and another by Herbert L. Clarke of London. The rooms were magnetic with charming associations.

A correspondent from a leading New York daily, commissioned to write of Mrs. Moulton's home, described her drawing-room as

"Long, high, and altogether spacious and dignified. A library opening from the rear increases the apparent length of the apart-

ment, so that it is a veritable salon; the
furnishings are of simple elegance in color
and design, and the whole scheme of decoration quiet and not ultra-modern.

"But in this attractive room are more treasures than one would dream of at first glance.
The fine paintings that are scattered here,
there, and everywhere, are all of them veritable
works of art, presented to Mrs. Moulton by
their painters; the etchings are autograph
copies from some of the best masters of
Europe. Almost every article of decoration,
it would seem, has a history. The books that
have overflowed from the dim recesses of the
library are mostly presentation copies in
beautiful bindings, with many a well-turned
phrase on their fly leaves written by authors
we all know and love.

"There could be no better guide through
all this treasure-house of suggestive material
than Mrs. Moulton herself. Without question she knows more English people of note
than does any other living American. As
she spreads out before the delighted caller
her remarkable collection of presentation photographs, she intersperses the exhibit with
brilliant off-hand descriptions of their originals
— the sort of word-painting that bookmen are
eager to hear in connection with their literary

idols. It is the real Swinburne she brings to
the mind's eye, with his extraordinary personal
appearance and his weird manners; the real
William Watson, profoundly in earnest and
varying in moods; the real George Egerton,
with her intensity and devotion to the higher
rights of womankind; the real Thomas Hardy
and George Meredith and Anthony Hope,
and the whole band of British authors, big
and little, whom she marshals in review and
dissects with unerring perception and the
keenest of wit. Anecdotes of all these per-
sonages flow from her tongue with a prodi-
gality that makes one long for the art of
shorthand to preserve them."

From this home in the early eighties the
daughter of the house was married to
Mr. William Henry Schaefer, of Charleston,
South Carolina. In her daughter's removal
to that Southern city, Mrs. Moulton's life
found an extension of interests. She made
frequent visits to Charleston before what
now came to be her annual spring sailings to
Europe. In her later years Mrs. Moulton
and her daughter and son-in-law often travelled together, though Mrs. Moulton's enjoyment centred itself more and more, as the
years went by, in her extensive and sympathetic

social life. Always was she pre-eminently the poet and the friend; and travel became to her the means by which she arrived at her desired haven, rather than was indulged in for its own sake. Yet the lovely bits of description which abound in her writings show that she journeyed with the poet's eye; as, for instance, this on leaving Rome:

"The deep blue Italian sky seemed warm with love and life, the fountains tossed high their white spray and flashed in the sunshine. Peasants were milking their goats at the foot of the Spanish Steps. Flower-girls had their arms full of fresh flowers, with the dew still on them, loading the air with fragrance."

Or this of Florence:

"I never cross the Ponte Vecchio, or Jewellers' Bridge, in Florence, without thinking of Longfellow's noble sonnet, and quoting to myself:

'Taddeo Gaddi built me,— I am old.'

Nor could I ever approach the superb equestrian statue of the Grand Duke Ferdinand without thinking of Browning's 'The Statue and the Bust.' 'The passionate pale lady's face' wrought by Lucca della Robbia no longer 'watches it from the square.'"

Just before her sailing in 1880 came this note from Mr. Longfellow:

Mr. Longfellow to Mrs. Moulton

CRAIGIE HOUSE, CAMBRIDGE, March 2, 1880.

DEAR MRS. MOULTON: . . . Yes, surely I will give you a letter to Lowell. I will bring it to you as soon as I am able to leave the house. . . . It was a great pleasure to meet you at Mrs. Ole Bull's, but I want to hear more about your visits to England, and whom you saw, and what you did. What is it? Is it the greater freedom one feels in a foreign country where no *Evening Transcript* takes note of one's outgoings and incomings? I can't attempt to explain it. Please don't get expatriated.

Ah, no, life is not all cathedrals and ruined castles, and other theatrical properties of the Old World. It is not all scenery, and within the four walls of home life is much the same everywhere.

Truly yours,
HENRY W. LONGFELLOW.

Of cathedrals and ruins she saw much, but people always interested her more than any inanimate things. She records her talks with one and another of the intellectual

with redoubled resolution if I feel that I have
the great public with me, as I had then (for
example) in the case of 'The New Magdalen.'
'Her Married Life,' in the second part, will
be essentially happy. But the husband and
wife — the world whose unchristian prejudices
and law they set at defiance will slowly under-
mine their happiness, and will, I fear, make
the close of the story a sad one."

The letter referred to was one of a long
series which Mrs. Moulton contributed to
the *New York Independent*. Many of these
papers were of marked literary value. A typical one was upon Mme. Desbordes-Valmore,
founded upon Sainte Beuve's memoir of that
interesting and unhappy French poet. Mrs.
Moulton characterizes Mme. Desbordes-Valmore as "the sad, sweet nightingale among
the singers of France, and as a tender, elegiac
poet" without equal. She closes with these
words:

"Mme. Valmore passed away in July of
1859. 'We shall not die,' she had said. In
that hour a gate was opened to some strange
land of light, some new dawning of glory,
and the holy saints, to whose fellowship she
belonged, received her into the very peace of
God."

Mrs. Moulton's witty essay on "The Gospel of Good Gowns" was one of this series in *The Independent*, and a fine paper of hers on Thoreau was widely quoted.

In a department which for some months she conducted under the title, "Our Society," in a periodical called *Our Continent*, Mrs. Moulton discoursed on manners, morals, and other problems connected with the conduct of life. The incalculable influence of the gentle, refined ideals that she persuasively imaged was a signal factor in the progress of life among the younger readers. Mrs. Moulton's ideal of the importance of manner was that of Tennyson's as expressed in his lines,—

> For manners are not idle, but the fruit
> Of loyal nature and of noble mind.

Many of these papers are included in Mrs. Moulton's book called "Ourselves and Our Neighbors," published in 1887. In one of these on "The Gospel of Charm" she says:

"So many new gospels are being preached, and that so strenuously, to the girls and women of the twentieth century, that I have wondered if there might not be a danger lest the Gospel of Charm should be neglected. And yet to my mind there are few teachings more important. I would advocate no charm on her part for information brought to her the following characteristic note, dated January, 1883:

Miss Alcott to Mrs. Moulton

"I have not the least objection to your writing a sketch of L. M. A. I shall feel quite comfortable in your hands. I have little material to give you; but in 'Little Women' you will find the various stages of my career and experience. Don't forget to mention that I don't like lion hunters, that I don't serve autophotos and biographies to the hundreds of boys and girls who ask, and that I heartily endorse Dr. Holmes' views on this subject."

To this volume the sketch of Mrs. Moulton herself was written by the graceful pen of Mrs. Harriet Prescott Spofford, who wrote with the sympathetic appreciation of the poet and close friend.

While on a visit to Spain in 1883,— and "Spain," she wrote, "is a word to conjure with,"—Mrs. Moulton made the acquaintance of Oswald Crawfurd the novelist, when he was in the diplomatic service. From his letters then and afterward might be taken many interesting passages, of which the following may serve as examples:

"There is another writer whose acquaintance
I have made, through his books, I mean, for
such interesting creatures as authors seldom
come to Portugal. We have to put up with
royalties, rich tourists, and wine merchants.
For me, the writers, the manipulators of ideas,
the shapers of them into human utterance,
are the important people of the age, as well as
the most agreeable to meet, in their books or
in life. This particularly pleasant one I have
just met is Frank Stockton. You will laugh
at the idea of my discovering what other people knew long ago, but it happens that I have
only just read his books. The three notes
that strike me in him are his perfect originality,
his literary dexterity, and his new and delicate
humor. I cannot say how he delighted me."

"We are going to give you Andrew Lang
to take you in [at the dinner] on Friday, and
on the other side you will have either James
Bryce or Mr. Chapman, the 'enterprising
young publisher' mentioned by Dickens.
Regarding Lang, I know no man who does so
many things so very well,— journalist, philolo-
gist, mythological researcher, — and to the
front in all these characters. To almost any
one but yourself I should call him a poet also.
His face is very refined and beautiful."

"I have been reading your poems again. You are as true a lyric artist as Landor or Herrick. I admire your sonnets,— they have a particular charm for me, and I am glad that you do not despise the old English form with the two last lines in rhyme. Shakespeare's, indeed, are so. I am almost inclined to think that for our rhymeless language, for an ear not attuned to the Italian perception for delicate rhyme of sounds, the strong emphasis on the ending couplet is right and good."

"I honestly like and admire the genius of Howells. I like his novels immensely, but his theories not at all."

The brief records in Mrs. Moulton's journal in these days suggest her crowded life of social enjoyment and literary work. On New Year's day of 1885 she notes having been the night before at a party at Mrs. Ole Bull's; and on that day she goes to a reception at the Howard Ticknors'; friends come to her in the evening. January second falls on a Friday, and as she is about to visit her daughter and son-in-law in Charleston, this is her last reception for the season. Naturally, it is a very full one, and while she does not chronicle the list of her guests, it is constructively easy to fancy that among them may have been Dr. Holmes,

LOUISE CHANDLER MOULTON

Page 122

Professor Horsford, the poet Aldrich and his lovely wife; Dean Hodges, always one of her most dearly esteemed friends; Mrs. Ole Bull, the Whipples, Oscar Fay Adams, Professor Lane of Harvard, Arlo Bates, in whose work, even then, she was taking great delight; Mrs. Kate Gannett Wells, Mrs. Julia Ward Howe, or her daughter, Mrs. Maud Howe Elliott; Mrs. Harriet Prescott Spofford; Mrs. Julius Eichberg and her brilliant daughter, Mrs. Anna Eichberg King (now Mrs. John Lane of London), — these and many others of her Boston circle who were habitués of her "Fridays," and seldom, indeed, was one of these receptions without some guests of special distinction who were visiting Boston. On one occasion it was Mr. and Mrs. Edmund Gosse of London; or again, Matthew Arnold; W. D. Howells was to be met there when in Boston; and not infrequently Colonel T. W. Higginson; Helen Hunt, whom Mrs. Moulton had long known; Mary Wilkins (now Mrs. Freeman), always cordially welcomed; Mrs. Clement Waters, the art writer; President Alice Freeman of Wellesley College (later Mrs. George Herbert Palmer); and Governor and Mrs. Claflin, at whose home Whittier was usually a guest during his sojourns in Boston, were among the familiar guests. Mr. Whittier could seldom be induced to appear at any large reception; but from Mrs. Moulton's early youth he had been one of her nearer friends, and his calls were usually for her alone.

Bliss Carman and Edgar Fawcett from New York were sometimes to be met in Mrs. Moulton's drawing-room; and there were also a group of Boston artists, — Arthur Foote who had set to music several of Mrs. Moultons, lyrics; B. J. Lang and his daughter, who had also set some of Mrs. Moulton's songs; the painters, I. M. Gaugengigl, Winthrop Pierce, John Enneking; Miss Porter and Miss Clarke, the editors of *Poet-Lore;* Caroline Ticknor, the young author whose work continued the literary traditions of her famous name; and often some of the clergy of Boston, — the Rev. Dr. Charles Gordon Ames, with Mrs. Ames, both of whom were among Mrs. Moulton's most dearly-prized friends; occasionally Rev. Dr. Edward Everett Hale, and Bishop Phillips Brooks; in a later decade, Rev. Dr. E. Winchester Donald, who succeeded Phillips Brooks as rector of Trinity; Rev. Bernard Carpenter, a brother of the Lord Bishop of Ripon; and beside the throngs of representative people who, at one time or another through some thirty years, were to be met at Mrs. Moulton's, the socially unknown guest received from the hostess the same cordial welcome. Her sympathies had little relation to social standing. No praise of the critics ever gave her more happiness than did a letter from a stranger in the West, written by a young girl who had for years been unable to move from her bed, telling of the blessed ministry of a poem by Mrs. Moulton, of which the first stanza runs:

> We lay us down to sleep,
> And leave to God the rest,
> Whether to wake and weep
> Or wake no more be best.

A book of Mr. Stedman's of which he sent to Mrs. Moulton a copy bore on its fly-leaf the inscription:

> My life-long, loyalist friend,
> My sister in life and song.

In the winter of 1885 the journal notes a visit to Mrs. Schaefer in Charleston, where amid all the festivities she finds time to send "four short stories and a poem" to various editors. On her way North she visited Washington, where dinners and receptions were given to her in private and in diplomatic circles. Then she went on to New York, and before sailing for Europe met Monsignor Capel at dinner, lunched with the Lawrence Barretts, attended Mr. Barrett's performance of "The Blot in the 'Scutcheon," which she found a "wonderful piece of acting," and at last sailed, as usual lavishly remembered with flowers and graceful tokens.

In Venice this year Mrs. Moulton wrote the charming pseudo-triolet,

IN VENICE ONCE.

In Venice once they lived and loved —
　　Fair women with their red gold hair —
Their twinkling feet to music moved,
In Venice where they lived and loved,
And all Philosophy disproved,
　　While hope was young and life was fair,
In Venice where they lived and loved.

It is interesting to feel in this a far suggestion of Browning's "A Toccata of Galuppi's," because so seldom does any echo of her contemporaries strike through Mrs. Moulton's verse.

With friends Mrs. Moulton visited Capri, Sorrento, Amalfi, Castellamare, Pompeii, and then went on to Rome. Here she passed the morning of her fiftieth birthday in the galleries of the Vatican. Friends made a *festa* of her birthday, with a birthday-cake and gifts; and she dined with the Storys, to go on later to one of Sir Moses Ezekiel's notable *musi-*

cales at his study in the Baths of Diocletian.
"The most picturesque of studios," she wrote,
"and a most cosmopolitan company, — at
least fifty ladies and gentlemen, representing
every civilized race. . . . All languages were
spoken. Pascarella, the Italian poet, recited.
. . . Professor Lunardi, of the Vatican library,
who has his Dante and Ariosto by heart, was
talking Latin to an American Catholic clergy-
man." Of this studio she gives a picturesque
description:

"Suspended from the lofty ceiling was a
hanging basket of flowers encircled by a score
of lights; while around the walls hundreds
of candles in antique sconces were burning,
throwing fitful gleams over marble busts and
groups of statuary. The frescoes on the walls
are fragments of the walls of Diocletian, and
the floor is covered with rich antique tiles
fifteen hundred years old. Eight elephants'
heads hold the candles that light the studio on
ordinary occasions. Two colossal forms claim
the attention of the visitor; one, the picture of
a herald, drawn by Sir. Moses, holds in his
right hand the shield of art; the other is the
figure of Welcome, holding in one hand a glass
of wine, while the other rests upon a shield.
The most striking and interesting work in the

studio is the group of Homer. The figure of
the poet is of heroic size, and he is represented
sitting on the seashore, reciting the Iliad,
and beating time with his hands; even in his
blindness, his face wears an expression that
seems to be looking into the future and down
through the ages of time. At his feet is seated
his guide, a youth with Egyptian features,
who accompanies Homer with strokes on the
lyre."

In the studio was also a bronze bust of
Liszt, the only one for which he ever sat, and
which Sir Moses modelled at the Villa d'Este.

After Rome came Florence, where Mrs.
Moulton was the guest of Mrs. Clara Erskine
Clement Waters, who had taken a villa in that
city. Among other people whom Mrs. Moulton met at this time was "Ouida," who un-
bent from her accustomed stiffness to Americans, and, yielding to the charm of her guest,
displayed her house and pets in a manner
which for her was almost without precedent.
Mrs. Waters gave a brilliant reception in her
honor; she was the guest of the Princess Kolt-
zoff Massalsky (Dora d'Istria), and she visited
Professor Fiske at the Villa Landor, where
she was "charmed by his wonderful library"
with its collections of the most notable edi-

tions of Dante and Petrarca; and she was entertained by Professor and Madame Villari.

From Florence she went to Aix-les-Bains. Then she passed to England.

In London she saw constantly almost everybody of note in literary circles. Her diary records visits to or from or meetings with the Lord Bishop of Winchester, Mrs. Bloomfield Moore, Lord Morley, Thomas Hardy, the Bishop of Ripon, Mr. Verschoyle of the *Fortnightly Review*, William Sharp, Frederick Wedmore, Sir Frederic and Lady Pollock, Dr. Furnival, and others, for a list too long to give entire. Her journal shows how full were her days.

"Mrs. Campbell-Praed came to lunch; a lot of callers in the afternoon, among them the Verschoyles, the Francillons, Mrs. Cashel-Hoey, Mrs. Fred Chapman, and Mrs. Anna Lea Merritt.

"Went to the Chapmans' to luncheon; met George Meredith. . . . Meredith is a very brilliant and agreeable man.

"Francillon to luncheon. A lovely letter from Oswald Crawfurd, praising Andrew Lang. . . . Went with Mrs. Marable to see Mrs. Sutherland Orr; a very charming person."

Herbert E. Clarke, whom in a letter to Professor Bates she described as "a wonderfully charming and fine fellow," accompanied a volume of his poems which he sent to her with these graceful dedicatory verses:

TO LOUISE CHANDLER MOULTON.

(WITH "VERSES ON THE HILLSIDE.")

Go forth, O little flower of song,
  To her who found you fair;
After a winter black as night,
I plucked you when spring's smile brought light,
And April's winds were blithe and strong,
  And Hope was in the air.

Poor stray of Autumn left to Spring,
  I send you forth to be
'Twixt us a pledge of happier hours;
Yea, though she hath far fairer flowers
Always at hand for gathering,
  Go forth undoubtingly.

For thou hast gained a happy meed,
  And wert thou weed or worse,
With her praise for a light above,
Many should find thee fair, and love
Though not for thine own sake indeed, —
  But her sake, O my verse.

Be weed or flower, and live or die,
  To me thou art more dear
Than all thy sister flowerets are,
O herald of the single star
That rose above the lowering sky
  Of my most hopeless year.

One particularly delightful day was that on which Mrs. Moulton attended a garden-party at Lambeth Palace as the guest of the Archbishop of Canterbury and Mrs. Benson. Another of the red-letter days was an afternoon with the Holman Hunts, in their rambling, fascinating house, filled with artistic treasures, when on the lawn a Hungarian orchestra played their national airs. Among the guests were Lewis Morris, Edwin Arnold, Hall Caine, Theodore Watts-Dunton, and many others who bore names well known. The diary records, too, a studio-reception given by Felix Moscheles, a coaching trip to Virginia Water; and so on for a round of gay doings which make it amazing that all this time Mrs. Moulton continued her literary work.

In the autumn Mrs. Moulton journeyed to Carlsbad, and there "made Lady Ashburton's acquaintance in the morning and sat up in the wood with her for a couple of hours." The acquaintance ripened into a warm friendship between the two, and Mrs. Moulton was often a guest at Lady Ashburton's place, Kent House, Knightsbridge. The sonnet "One Afternoon" is the memory of this first meeting written at Carlsbad a year after.

On her return to America in the autumn, Mrs. Moulton went to Pomfret to visit her mother. While there she heard from Miss Guiney of the death of a young poet, James Berry Bensel, of whom she wrote to Oscar Fay Adams as follows:

Mrs. Moulton to Mr. Adams

28 Rutland Square, Sunday.

MY DEAR FRIEND: Your letter just received draws my very heart out in sympathy. I wish you were here, that I could tell you all the feelings that it brought, for I know what it is to lose my dearest friend. Louise Guiney said to me when she came Friday afternoon: "I have something to tell you. Bensel is dead. His brother has written me." And I was not myself all the afternoon. I could not put aside the thought that pleaded for my tears. And I grieved that I had not yet written to him about his book. I find such fine things in it. Come back and let us grieve for him together, — not that I grieve as you do who loved him so, but I do understand all you feel, and I felt his death very unusually, myself. I wish, oh, how I wish, we could call him back to life, and give him health, and the strength to work, and more favorable conditions. But we do not know but that he may now be rejoicing somewhere in a great gain, beyond our vision. He has gone where our

vision cannot find or our fancy follow him;
but he must either be better off in a new birth
or else so deeply at rest that no pain can
pierce him where he is. Good-bye and God
bless you.   Yours most truly,
                    LOUISE CHANDLER MOULTON.

The Boston winters were full always with
social and literary interests. The relations of
Mrs. Moulton to the writers of her circle were
indicated when on her sailing in the spring of
one of the late eighties a post-bag was arranged
which was delivered to her in mid-ocean. The
idea originated with Miss Marian Boyd Allen,
and among the contents were a manuscript
book of poems for every day by Bliss Carman;
poems by Clinton Scollard, Arlo Bates, Willis
Boyd Allen, Minot J. Savage, Celia Thaxter,
the Rev. Bernard Carpenter, Gertrude Hall,
Mary Elizabeth Blake, and Hezekiah Butter-
worth; a silver vinaigrette from Professor
James Mills Pierce; a book from Mrs. Clara
Erskine Clement Waters; two charming draw-
ings from Winthrop Pierce; with notes from
Nora Perry, Colonel T. W. Higginson, and
others. Miss Guiney addressed as her "Chief
Emigrant and Trans-Atlantic Gadder, Most
Ingenious Poet, and Queen of Hearts." Col-
onel Higginson wrote:

T. W. Higginson to Mrs. Moulton

CAMBRIDGE, May 3, 1887.

DEAR FRIEND: I gladly join with others in this mid-ocean post-bag. I hope you will take your instalments of friendship in as many successive days. Few American women, — perhaps none, — have succeeded in establishing such a pleasant intermedian position before English and American literature as have you, and as the ocean does not limit your circle of friends, it seems very proper that we on this side should stretch our hands to you across it. As one of your oldest and best friends, I wish you not only "many happy returns," but one, at least, in the autumn.

Ever cordially,

T. W. HIGGINSON.

On the other side of the Atlantic Philip Bourke Marston and his friend William Sharp greeted her return to London in three sonnets.

Philip Bourke Marston to Mrs. Moulton

UNDESCRIED. — TO L. C. M.

When from her world, new world, she sailed away,
    Right out into the sea-winds and the sea,
    Did no foreshadowing of good to be
Surprise my heart? That memorable day

Did I as usual rise, think, do, and say
  As on a day of no import to me?
  Did hope awake no least low melody?
Send forth no spell my wandering steps to stay?
  Oh, could our souls catch music of the things
From some lone height of being undescried,
  Then had I heard the song the sea-wind sings
The waves; and through the strain of storm and tide, —
  As soft as sleep and pure as lovely springs, —
Her voice wherein all sweetnesses abide.

William Sharp to Mrs. Moulton

ANTICIPATED FRIENDSHIP

Friend of my friend! as yet to me unknown,
  Shall we twain meeting meet and care no more?
  Already thou hast left thy native shore,
And to thine ears the laughter and the moan
Of the strange sea by night and day unknown,
  Its thunder and its music and its roar;
  A few days hence the journey will be o'er,
And I shall know if hopes have likewise flown.
As one hears by the fire a father tell
  His eager child some tales of fairy land,
Where no grief is and no funereal bell,
  But thronging joys and many a happy band;
So do I hope fulfillment will be well,
  And not scant grace, with cold, indifferent hand.

AFTER MEETING

Friend of my friend, the looked-for day has come,
  And we have met: to me, at least, a day
Memorable: no hopes have flown away.
  Bad fears lie broken, stricken henceforth dumb:
In the thronged room, and in the ceaseless hum
  Of many voices, I heard one voice say

A few brief words, — but words that did convey
  A subtle breath of friendship, as in some
Few scattered leaves the rose still gives her scent.
  Thy hand has been in mine, and I this night
Have seen thine eyes reach answer eloquent
  To unseen questions winged for eager flight.
And when, at last, our Philip and I went,
  I knew that I had won a fresh delight.

The following letter from Mr. Sharp explains itself in this cluster of greetings:

William Sharp to Philip Bourke Marston

19 ALBERT STREET, REGENT'S PARK.

DEAR PHILIP: I could n't be bothered going out anywhere, as you suggested, and an hour or two ago I was able to complete a second sonnet for the two on "Anticipated Friendship" addressed to Mrs. Moulton. I told you how much I liked her, and what a relief it was to find my hopes not disappointed. In reading these sonnets (at least, the second one) remember the dolorous condition I am in, and have mercy on all short-comings that therein abound; and, please, if you think the spirit of thankfulness in them not sufficient to overbalance all deficiencies, throw them in the fire without showing them to their unconscious inspirer, and thus earn the future gratitude of

        Your loving friend,

            WILLIAM SHARP.

In February of 1887 Philip Bourke Marston died. He bequeathed to Mrs. Moulton his books and manuscripts, and many autographs of great interest and value. Among them was the first page of the original manuscript of the first great chorus in "Atalanta in Calydon" corrected in Swinburne's own hand. Marston requested that she should be his literary executor. Speaking of this work some years later, Mrs. Moulton said:

"When I first knew the Marstons they were a group of five, — dear old Dr. Marston, his son, Philip Bourke Marston, his unmarried daughter Cecily, his married daughter Mrs. Arthur O'Shaughnessy, and her husband. I edited a volume of selections by O'Shaughnessy; and I was named by Mr. Marston, in his will, as his literary executor. I brought out after his death a volume whose contents had not been hitherto included in any book, and which I called 'A Last Harvest.' Then I put all his flower-poems together (as he had long wished to do) in a volume by themselves, which was entitled 'Garden Secrets.' Finally I have brought out a collected edition of his poems, including the three volumes published before his death, and the ones I had compiled after he died.

"Ah, you may well call his life tragic. He was only three years old when he lost his sight. He was educated orally, but his knowledge of literature was a marvel. The poets of the past were his familiar friends, and he could repeat Swinburne's poems by the hour. To recite Rossetti's 'House of Life' was one of the amusements of his solitary days. But he longed, beyond all things, to be constantly in touch with the world — to know what every year, every month, was producing. 'Can you fancy what it is,' he would say to me sometimes, 'to be just walled in with books that you are dying to read, and to have them as much beyond your reach as if they were the other side of the world?' Yet he had, despite his sad fate, the gayest humor — the most naturally cheerful temperament; he could be so merry with his friends — so happy 'when there was anything to be happy about.' Of his work 'Garden Secrets' is uniquely charming. Rossetti once wrote him, in a letter of which I am the fortunate possessor, that he had been reading these 'Garden Secrets,' the evening before, to William Bell Scott, the poet-artist, and adds, 'Scott fully agreed with me that they were worthy of Shakespeare, in his subtlest lyrical moods.' Some of the best critics in London declared that the author of

'Song-Tide' (Marston's first volume) should, by virtue of this one book, take equal rank with Swinburne, Morris, and Rossetti. Certainly his subsequent volumes fully sustained the promise of this first one, and I feel that when Philip Bourke Marston died, at the age of thirty-seven, on the fourteenth of February, 1887, England lost one of her noblest and subtlest poets — one whose future promise it were hard to overrate. Sometimes I think I care most for some of his sonnets; then the subtle beauty of his lyrics upbraids me, — and I hardly know which to choose. Take him all in all, he seems to me a poet whom future generations will recognize and remember."

Regarding the death of Mr. Marston, Mr. Whittier wrote to the friend who had brought so much brightness into the life of the blind poet:

Mr. Whittier to Mrs. Moulton

CENTRE HARBOR, N. H., 7th month, 1887.

MY DEAR FRIEND, LOUISE CHANDLER MOULTON: It was very kind in thee to send thy admirable little book and most welcome letter. We have read thy wise and charming essay up here among the hills, and under the shadow of the pines, with hearty approval.

It was needed, and will do a great deal of good to young people, in the matter of manners and morals.

It seems a very long time since I had the great pleasure of seeing thee, or of hearing directly from thee. I meant to have been in Boston in the early spring, and looked forward to the satisfaction of meeting thee, but I was too ill to leave home, and I felt a real pang of regret when I learned of thy departure. I am now much better, but although I cannot say with the Scotch poet that

> " the years hang o'er my back
> And bend me like a muckle pack,"

I must still confess that they are getting uncomfortably heavy. But I have no complaint to make. My heart is as warm as ever, and love and friendship as dear.

I was pained by the death of thy friend, Philip Marston. It must be a comfort to thee to know that thy love and sympathy made his sad lot easier to be borne. He was one who needed love, and I think he was one to inspire it also.

My old and comfortable hotel at Centre Harbor, where I have been a guest for forty years, was burned to ashes a few days ago, after we came away. But we are now in good, neat quarters at a neat farm house, with large cool rooms on the border of the lovely lake.

Good-bye, dear friend! While enjoying thy many friends in London, do not forget thy friends here.

> Ever affectionately thy old friend,
> JOHN G. WHITTIER.

Herbert E. Clarke, the warm and intimate friend of Marston, touchingly alludes to his death in this sonnet.

TO LOUISE CHANDLER MOULTON.

Ah, friend, the die is cast, — life turns to prose.
  My way lies onward — dusty, hot, and bare,
  Through the wide plain under the noonday glare, —
A sordid path whereby no singer goes;
For yon the cloudy crags — the stars and snows —
  Limitless freedom of ethereal air
  And pinnacles near heaven.   On foot I fare,
Halting foredoomed, and toward what goal who knows?
But though the singer who may sing no more
  Bears ever in his heart a smothered fire,
I give Fate thanks: nor these my pangs deplore,
  Seeing song gave first rewards beyond desire —
Your love, O Friend, and his who went before,
  The sightless singer with his silver lyre.

LONDON, 1st August, 1888.

To Arlo Bates, Mrs. Moulton, reading this, repeated the closing line with a touching tenderness, and then without further word laid the manuscript aside.

In the middle years of the eighties Mrs. Moulton began to send to the *Boston Herald* a series of literary letters from London, and these she continued for a number of years. She was especially well fitted for the undertaking by her wide acquaintance with English writers, her unusual power of appreciating work not yet endorsed by public approval, and her sympathetic instinct for literary quality. The work, while arduous, gave her pleasure, chiefly because it provided opportunity for her to give encouragement and aid to others, and to help to make better known writers and work not yet appreciated in America. "I am sending a literary letter each week to the *Boston Herald*," she writes Mr. Stedman. "It is hard work, but it gives me the pleasure of expressing myself about the current literature. I believe the letters are accounted a success."

Many were the letters of gratitude which came to her from those of whom she had written. The sympathetic quality of her approval, so rarely found in combination with critical judgment, made her praise especially grateful. Not only did she interest and enlighten her reading public, but she encouraged and inspired those of whom she wrote.

Other letters of grateful recognition came

Venus After Burne Jones.
(After a visit to the Grosvenor
Gallery in 1878.)

Pallid with too much longing,
    (White with passion and prayer,
Goddess of Love & Beauty,
    She sits in the picture there.

Sits with her dark eyes seeking
    Something more subtle still
Than the old delights of loving
    Her measureless days to fill.

She has loved and been loved so often
    In the long, immortal years

                    (over)

That she tires of the worn-out rapture,
  Sickens of hopes and fears.

No joys nor sorrows move her —
  Done with her ancient pride —
The crown she found too heavy
  She has wearily cast aside.

Clothed in her scarlet splendour,
  Bright with her glory of hair
Sad that she is not mortal,
  Eternally sad and fair,

Longing for joys she knows not,
  Athirst with a vain desire,
There she sits in the picture,
  Daughter of foam and fire.

  Louise Chandler Moulton

now and then from artists of whose work she
had written in verse. After a visit to the studio of Burne-Jones in London she was inspired to write the admirable and subtle lyric
"Laus Veneris," upon his picture of that
name.

> Pallid with too much longing,
>   White with passion and prayer,
> Goddess of love and beauty,
>   She sits in the picture there, —
>
> Sits with her dark eyes seeking
>   Something more subtle still
> Than the old delights of loving
>   Her measureless days to fill.
>
> She has loved and been loved so often,
>   In the long, immortal years,
> That she tires of the worn-out rapture,
>   Sickens of hopes and fears.
>
> No joys or sorrows move her,
>   Done with her ancient pride;
> For her head she found too heavy
>   The crown she has cast aside.
>
> Clothed in her scarlet splendor,
>   Bright with her glory of hair,
> Sad that she is not mortal, —
>   Eternally sad and fair, —
>
> Longing for joys she knows not,
>   Athirst with a vain desire,
> There she sits in the picture,
>   Daughter of foam and fire.

It is not to be wondered that the artist wrote
in warm acknowledgment:

Mr. Burne-Jones to Mrs. Moulton

" I think you must know how glad all workers
are of such sympathy as you have shown me,
and I don't know of any other reward that
one ever sets before one's self that can be
compared for a moment with the gratified
sense of being understood. It's like hearing
one's tongue in a foreign land. I do assure
you I worked all the more confidently the day
your letter came. Confidence and courage
do often fail, and when all the senses are
thoroughly tired with work, and the heart
discouraged, a tribute like the one you sent
me is a real refreshment."

During all these years Mrs. Moulton's
mastery of technical form, and especially her
efficiency in the difficult art of the sonnet,
had steadily increased. George H. Boker
wrote to her: "In your ability to make the
sonnet all it should be you surpass all your
living, tuneful sisterhood." Certainly after
the death of Mrs. Browning no woman writing English verse could be named as Mrs.
Moulton's possible rival in the sonnet save
Christina Rossetti, and no woman in America,

if indeed any man, could rank with her in this.

In many of Mrs. Moulton's sonnets is found a subtle, elusive suggestion of spiritual things, as if the poet were living between the two worlds of the seen and the unseen, with half-unconscious perceptions, strange and swift, of the unknown. With this spiritual outlook are mingled human love and longing. The existence of any genuine poet must be dual. He holds two kinds of experience, one that has been lived in outward life; the other, not less real, that has been lived intuitively and through the power of entering, by sympathy, into other lives and varied qualities of experience.

Mrs. Moulton's imaginative work, both in her stories and her poems, suggests this truth in a remarkable degree. Her nature presents a sensitive surface to impressions. She has the artist's power of selection from these, and the executive gift to combine, arrange, and present. Thus her spiritual receptivity gives to her work that deep vitality, that sense of soul in it that holds the reader, while her artistic touch moulds her rare and exquisite beauty of finished design.

In 1889 Mrs. Moulton published another volume of collected tales, the last that she

10

"Louise Guiney came in to help me look over my poems. We worked till night, then went to the Cecilia concert to hear Maida Lang's quartet."

"Such a busy morning! Polished off a rondel to send to the *Independent*. Read *Herald* proof; wrote letters. This afternoon pleasant guests,— Mrs. Ole Bull, Mr. Clifford, Percival Lowell, and others."

[In New York.] "Went over to Brooklyn and gave a Browning reading. . . . Met the Russian Princess Engalitcheff. Lunched at Mrs. Field's with the Princess and Mr. and Mrs. Locke Richardson. Went in the evening to the Gilders.'"

"Wrote a little. . . . Mrs. [John T.] Sargent and sweet Nellie Hutchinson called in the forenoon; and in the afternoon ten people, including Stedman."

[In London.] "Worked on poems in forenoon. Had a lovely basket of flowers from dear old Mr. Greenough. Gave a little dinner at night at the Grand Hotel, to the Oswald Crawfurds, Sir Bruce Seton, Mrs. Trubner, and Mr. Greenough."

Extracts of this sort might be multiplied, and they explain why it was that amid so much apparent preoccupation with social affairs Mrs. Moulton kept steadily her place as a literary worker. Her genuine and abiding love for letters was the secret of her ability thus to enter with zest into the pleasures of life without losing her power of artistic production.

Among the records of the year 1889 is this touching entry, with the date April 27, at the close of a visit to her mother:

"Poor mother's last words to me were: 'I love you better than anything in this world. You are my first and last thought. Believe it, for it is the *truth*.'"

In London this summer Mrs. Moulton was considering a title for a new volume of poems, and had asked advice of William Winter. He chanced to be in England at the time, and wrote at once:

Mr. Winter to Mrs. Moulton

No. 13 UPPER PHILLIMORE PLACE,
HIGH STREET, KENSINGTON,
August 14, 1889.

DEAR LOUISE: Your letter has just come. Business affairs brought me suddenly to town. I will seek to see you as soon as they can be disposed of, Saturday or Sunday, perhaps.

indeed, as they were mostly dated by a month only) is, in any case, negligible in importance.

The extracts chosen deal almost exclusively with literary matters. The only son of Professor Bates, in his twentieth year, afterward the author of "A Madcap Cruise," whom Mrs. Moulton playfully called "Prince Oric," and to whom in his sixth year she wrote a delicious sonnet under that title, is alluded to, as well as is his mother, who wrote over the pen-name Eleanor Putnam.

Mrs. Moulton to Arlo Bates

". . . Thanks for the charming book. My love to the sweetest wife I know. Thank her for her letter. . . ."

". . . Your letter about Marston's songs came to me when he and William Sharp happened to be passing the evening with me. I read it aloud, to Mr. Marston's great delight. It quite went to his heart. . . . I am so sorry I shall not find you and Mrs. Bates where you were last year. That desperate flirtation with Master Oric is off entirely. . . ."

". . . I have just been reading 'Childe Roland,' and it baffles me, as it has so often done before. I feel less sure that I understand it than any other of Browning's poems.

Is the Black Tower Death, do you think?
But what a wonderful poem it is! I suppose
spiritual judgments concern themselves with
spiritual states. . . ."

". . . I am delighted with what you say of
Mr. Marston's poem in *Harper's*, because I
think the poem too subtle and delicate to be
appreciated, save by the very elect; and I am
also delighted because what you said gave
him so much pleasure. Marston said of you,
'What a wonderful psychological vein, almost
as powerful as that of Browning, runs through
many of the poems of Mr. Bates.' . . ."

". . . I am so eager to see your novel of
artistic Boston. 'The Pagans,' — a capital
title. I am glad you have had the courage
to tell the truth in it as you see it. I don't
see it quite as you do, I fancy, but I am thankful when any one has the courage of his opinions, for it seems to me that the English and
American writers are just now very much
like cats standing on the edge of a stream,
and afraid to put in their feet. They say what
they think is expected of them to say, and
they reserve the truth for the seasons when
they enter their closets and shut the door on
all the world. I think there is more hypocrisy
in novels than in religion."

" . . . I am ashamed that two weeks have gone by since I received your noble book, 'Told in the Gate.' I have not been so neglectful of it as it seems. I have not only taken my own pleasure in it, but I have shown it to other poets who are interested in knowing what is being done in America. It is a beautiful book externally — how beautiful it is internally I am sure the world of readers will eagerly perceive; but never one of them can love it more than I do. Even in print it is hard for me to say which poem I prefer. There is not one among them that is not well done from the point of art, and thrillingly interesting as a story. The lyrics star the book like gems. They sing themselves over and over to my listening mind. . . . I feel a glow of exultant pride that the author is my friend. I am proud and glad to have my name inscribed in a volume I so admire and love. I am enjoying London as I always do. . . . I go toward the end of August to pay some visits in Scotland, and then to visit Lady Ashburton in Hampshire and after that to Paris. I enclose some foreign stamps for the young Prince. . . . Your poems are among the pleasures of my life."

Of the sonnets of Mr. Bates Mrs. Moulton wrote:

" . . . Dante breathed through the sonnet the high aspirations of that love which shaped and determined his soul's life. By sonnets it was that Petrarch wedded immortally his name to that of his ever-wooed, never-won Laura of Avignon. Strong Michael Angelo wrote sonnets for that noble lady, Vittoria Colonna, whose hand he kissed only after Death had kissed the soul from her pure lips.

" The one personal intimacy with Shakespeare to which any of his worshippers have been admitted is such as comes from loving study of his sonnets, in 'sessions of sweet, silent thought.' The sonnets of Elizabeth Barrett Browning burned with the pure flame of her perfect love. In the sonnets of 'The House of Life' Rossetti commemorated that love and loss so passionate and so abiding that it seemed to him the whole of life. In the sonnets of 'Song-Tide' Marston sang the praises of his early love, as in those of 'All In All' he bewailed her loss; and his sonnets of later years throb like a tell-tale heart with the profoundest melancholy out of whose depths a human soul ever cried for pity.

" Such and thus intimate have been the revelations made through this form of verse — so rigid, yet so plastic and so human.

" To the list of these sonneteers who have

thus sounded the deepest depths of love and sorrow, the name of Arlo Bates has now been added, by the publication of his noble and sincere 'Sonnets in Shadow.' Born of one man's undying pain, these sonnets at once become, through the subtlety of their research into the innermost depths of human emotion, the property and the true expression of all souls who have loved and suffered.

"A few of us know, personally, the rare charm, the exquisite loveliness, of her thus royally honored and passionately lamented; and all of us who read can feel that thus and thus our own hearts might be wrung by such a loss — that in us, also, if we have souls at all, such sorrow might bear fruit in kindred emotion, even though for want of words our lips be dumb. It seems to me that it is the dumb souls — who feel all that the poet has sung, and yet cannot break the silence with a cry — who owe the deepest debt to this, their interpreter."

Mrs. Moulton to Mr. Bates

"OCTOBER 27, 1889.

"I have been passing this rainy afternoon with your sonnets. I had read some of them more than once before, but this afternoon I

have been quite alone save for their good
company. I have read the strong, noble
sequence through, from first to last, enjoying
them more than ever. I like every one of
them, but I had a pencil and paper by me
and put down the numbers that most moved
me. I see that my list is not short; do you
care to see what it includes? It begins with
the beautiful sonnet of dedication; then the
first, with its wonderful procession of the gray
days passing the torpid soul, and laying
their 'curious fingers, chill and numb,'
upon its wounds. Then the sixth, with the

> " . . . drowned sailors, lying lank and chill
> Under the sirupy green wave.

And the fifteenth with its visions of love.

> " Never can joy surmise how long are sorrow's hours,

ought to be, like certain lines of Wordsworth,
among the immortal quotations. I think your
sonnets noble alike in thought and in execution.
They can have no more faithful lover than I
am; and I do believe that if there is anything
in which my opinion has any value, it is on
the form of poetry. I love it so sincerely
and I have studied it so devotedly. . . .

" . . . Mrs. Spofford has been to stay over
Sunday with me and I read through to her
your new volume of poems, with the excep-

tion of 'The Lilies of Mummel See,' which she read to me. I think you would be pleased, could you know how much we both enjoyed and admired the book. To my mind, ' Under the Beech Tree' is the finest romantic drama of the time. I like it far better than I do 'Colombe's Birthday,' much as I like that. Mrs. Spofford is quite wild with enthusiasm about 'The Gift.' She said the last line,

"His heart is still mine, beating warm in my grave,

is not only the finest line in your book, but the finest line that has been written by any one in a score of years."

" . . . Your suggestion as to national characteristics of women struck me as a curious coincidence with the fact that the editor of the *Fortnightly* has just asked me to write an article on American and English women, contrasting and comparing them, and discussing their differences. But the differences seem to me individual, not national.

" Thanks for your suggestion about the sonnet.

" Break through the shining, splendid ranks

seems to me simpler and more forcible, but then this involves the 'I pray,' to which you greatly object.

"Break through their splendid militant array:

"I'll copy both, and see what you think. On the whole, I like yours better.

"I have been arranging books all the afternoon, and I am so tired that I wish I had the young prince here, or such another,— only there is no other."

The same to the same

"DEAR PAGAN: I am on page 238 of 'The Puritans,' and I pause to say how piteously cruel is your portrait of ——. Sargent, at his best, was never so relentlessly realistic. I pity Fenton so desperately I can hardly bear it. Why do I sympathize so with him when he is so little worthy? Is it your fault, or mine? I believe I am not pitiless enough to write novels, even if I had every other qualification.

"Your character of Fenton is admirably studied. It is worthy of the author of 'The Pagans' and 'A Wheel of Fire.'"

". . . I have finished reading 'The Puritans,' — all the duties of life neglected till I came to the end. I have not been so interested in a book for ages. I am especially interested in the conflict of the souls between degrees of agnosticism. It is the keenest longing of my life to know what is truth."

"I have reason to be grateful for your birthday, since I find you one of the most interesting persons I have ever had the happiness to know."

"I have just finished reading 'The Diary of a Saint,' and I cannot wait an hour to tell you how very greatly I admire it. It has been said that all the stories were told. You prove how untrue is this statement, — for your story, or anything like it, has never been told before. It is absolutely unique and original. . . . I am so interested in every page of the book that I have an impatient desire to know all the spiritual experiences that lead to it."

"Just now at Les Voirons (Haute Savoie) I have found a sort of hilltop paradise. Four thousand and more feet above the sea level, the air is like balm, and the views indescribably lovely. I have never seen Mont Blanc half so well. It is far more wonderful than the view from Chamounix. And just now at night the white ghost of a young moon hangs above it, in a pale, clear sky, and the lesser peaks all around shimmer in the moonlight. This hotel is ten climbing miles from any railroad station. You can buy nothing here but postage stamps."

In a characteristic letter from Rome, Richard Greenough, the sculptor, says:

Mr. Greenough to Mrs. Moulton

"The sidereal certainty of your movements impresses me. It reminds me of the man who ordered his dinner in England a year in advance, and when the time came he was there to eat it. . . . Do I feel sure of a life after this? Was ever a note charged with such heavy ballast? To attempt an answer would take a volume, — to give an answer would require a conscience. . . . While reading Cicero's Tusculan Disputations 'On Grief,' I found a quotation from Sophocles that reminds me of your loss in Philip's death.

> "No comforter is so endowed with wisdom
> That while he soothes another's heavy grief,
> If altered fortune turns on him her blow,
> He will not bend beneath the sudden shock
> And spurn the consolation he had given.

"I wonder if you know how poetic you are? Do what you may, — read, write, or talk, you make real life seem ideal, and ideal life seem real. Your sweet 'After Death' is above all praise."

On the appearance of "Robert Elsmere" Mrs. Moulton read it with the greater inter-

11

est in that, as has already been noted, her own mind constantly reverted to religious problems. Writing to Mrs. Humphry Ward to congratulate her on the achievement, she received the following reply:

Mrs. Ward to Mrs. Moulton

LONDON, June 20, 1888.

DEAR MRS. MOULTON: Thanks for your interesting letter *in re* Robert Elsmere. There is no answer merely to the problems of evil and suffering except that of an almost blind trust. I see dimly that evil is a condition of good. Heredity and environment are awful problems. They are also the lessons of God.

Sincerely yours,

MARY A. WARD.

The publication in 1889 of the collection of poems entitled "In the Garden of Dreams" added greatly to Mrs. Moulton's standing as a poet. On the titlepage were the lines of Tennyson:

> Not wholly in the busy world, nor quite
> Beyond it, blooms the garden that I love.

The book contained a group of lyrics "To French Tunes," which showed that Mrs. Moulton had responded to the fashion for

the old French forms of rondel, rondeau,
triolet, and so on which in the eighties prevailed among London singers. They showed
her facility in manipulating words in metre
and were all graceful and delicate; but she
was a poet of emotion too genuine and feeling
too strong to be at her best in these artificial
and constrained measures. She wrote a few
in later years, which were included in the
volume called "At the Wind's Will," but although they were praised she never cared for
them greatly or regarded them as counting
for much in her serious work. The book as a
whole showed how the natural lyric singer
had developed into the fine and subtle artist.
The noblest portion of the collection, as in
her whole poetic work, was perhaps in the
sonnets; but throughout the volume the music
of the lines was fuller and freer, the thought
deeper, the emotion more compelling than in
her earlier work. With this volume Mrs.
Moulton took her place at the head of living
American poets, or, as an English critic
phrased it, "among the true poets of the
day."

The voice of the press was one of unanimous praise on both sides of the Atlantic.
The privately expressed criticisms of the members of the guild of letters were no less in

accord.   Mrs.   Spofford   said   of   "Waiting Night":

"It is a perfect thing. The wings of flying are all through it. It is fine, and free, and beautiful as the 'Statue and the Bust.' It is high, and sweet, and touching."

Dr. Holmes to Mrs. Moulton

296 BEACON ST.,
December 29, 1889.

MY DEAR MRS. MOULTON: I thank you most cordially for sending me your beautiful volume of poems. They tell me that they are breathed from a woman's heart as plainly as the fragrance of a rose reveals its birthplace. I have read nearly all of them — a statement I would not venture to make of most of the volumes I receive, the number of which is legion, and I cannot help feeling flattered that the author of such impassioned poems should have thought well enough of my own productions to honor me with the kind words I find on the blank leaf of a little book that seems to me to hold leaves torn out of the heart's record.

Believe me, dear Mrs. Moulton,
Faithfully yours,
O. W. HOLMES.

2 9/6 Beacon St. Dec. 29th
1889.

My dear Mrs. Moulton,

I thank most cordially
for lending me your beautiful
volume of poems. They tell
me that they are heathed
from a woman's heart as plain
as the fragrance of the rose
reveals its birth-place. I have
read most of them — a statement
I would not venture to make
of most of the volumes of poems
I receive — the number of which
is legion, — and I cannot help

feeling flattered that the author
of such impassioned poems should
have thought well enough of my own
productions to honor me with
the kind words I met on the blank
leaf of a little book that seems
to me to hold the heart's leaves
 ... out of her heart's blood.

Believe me, dear Mrs. Moulton
Faithfully Yours
O W Holmes.

Dr. Rolfe to Mrs. Moulton

CAMBRIDGE, Christmas, 1889.

DEAR MRS. MOULTON: How can I thank you enough for giving me a free pass to your "Garden of Dreams" with its delightful wealth of violets, fresh and sweet, lilies and roses, rosemary, and Elysian asphodel, and every flower that sad embroidery weaves? Put your ear down close and let me whisper very confidentially, — tell it not at our meetings at the Brunswick, publish it not in the streets of Boston! that I like your delicate and fragrant blossoms better than some of the hard nuts that the dear, dead Browning has given us in his "Asolando." Sour critics may tell us that the latter will last longer, — they are tough enough to endure, — but I doubt not that old Father Time, — who is not destitute of taste, withal, — will press some of your charming flowers between his ponderous chronicles, where their lingering beauty and sweetness will delight the appreciation of generations far distant. So may it be!

Luckily, one may wander at will with impunity in your lovely garden, even if he has as bad a cold as at present afflicts and stupefies your friend, though he may enjoy these all the more when he recovers his wonted good

Let them bear thought of me,
  With pleasant memories
To touch the heart of thee,
  From over-sea.

A little way it is for love to flee,
  Love winged with memories,
Hither to thither over-sea.

CHAPTER VI

1890–1895

And this is the reward. That the ideal shall be real to thee, and the impressions of the actual world shall fall like summer rain, copious, but not troublesome. . . . Doubt not, O Poet, but persist. — EMERSON.

> Onward the chariot of the Untarrying moves;
>   Nor day divulges him nor night conceals.
>   WILLIAM WATSON.

> They are winged, like the viewless wind,
>   These days that come and go. — L. C. M.

MRS. MOULTON'S morning-room was on the second floor, its windows looking into the green trees of Rutland Square. In one corner was her desk, in the centre a table always piled with new books, many of which were autographed copies from their authors, and around the walls were low bookcases filled with her favorite volumes. Above these hung pictures, and on their tops were photographs and mementos. The mantel was attractive with pretty bric-a-brac, largely gifts. Between the two front windows was her special table filled with the immediate letters of the day, and by it her own chair in which, on mornings, she was quite sure to be found by the little group of friends privileged to familiar intimacy.

No allusion to these delightful talks with Mrs. Moulton in her morning-room could be complete without mention of her faithful and confidential maid, Katy, whom all the frequenters of the house regarded with cordial friendliness as an important figure in the household life. It was Katy who knew to a shade the exact degree of greeting for the unending procession of callers, from the friends dearest and nearest, to the wandering minstrels who should have been denied, though they seldom were. It was Katy who surrounded the gracious mistress of the establishment with as much protection as was possible; but as Mrs. Moulton's sympathies were unbounded, while her time and strength had their definite limits, it will be seen that Katy's task was often difficult.

The informal lingerings in Mrs. Moulton's morning-room were so a part of the "dear days" that "have gone back to Paradise" that without some picture of them no record of her Boston life could be complete. The first mail was an event, and to it Mrs. Moulton gave her immediate attention after glancing through the morning paper with her coffee and roll. Her correspondence increased with every season, and while it was a valued part of her social life, it yet became a very serious tax on her time and energy. There were letters from friends and from strangers; letters from the great and distinguished, and from the obscure; and each and all received from her the same impartial consideration. Every conceivable human problem, it would seem, would be laid before her. Her name was sought for all those things for which the patroness is invented; there were not wanting those who desired her advice, her encouragement, her practical aid in finding, perhaps, a publisher for their hitherto rejected MSS. with an income insured; and they wanted her photograph, her autograph, her biography in general; a written "sentiment" which they might, indeed, incorporate into their own concoctions by way of adornment; or they frankly wanted her autograph with the provision that it should be appended to a check, presumably of imposing dimensions, — all these, and a thousand other requests were represented in her letters, quite aside from the legitimate correspondence of business and friendship. With all these she dealt with a generous consideration whose only defect was perhaps a

too ready sympathy. Her familiar friends
might sometimes try to restrain her response.
"It is an imposition!" one might unfeelingly
exclaim. "God made them," she would reply.
And to the insinuation that the Divine Power
had perhaps little to do in the creation of professional bores and beggars, she would smile
indulgently, but she usually insisted that it
"was n't right" to turn away from any appeal, although, of course, all appeals were not
to be granted literally. In vain did one be-
seech her to remember Sir Hugo's advice to
Daniel Deronda: "Be courteous, be obliging,
Dan, but don't give yourself to be melted
down for the tallow trade." She always insisted that even to be unwisely imposed upon
was better than to refuse one in real need;
and her charities — done with such delicacy
of tender helpfulness that for them charity is
too cold a name — were most generous. Her
countless liberal benefactions, moreover, were
of the order less easy than the mere signing
of checks, for into them went her personal
sympathy. She helped people to help themselves in the most thoughtful and lovely
ways.

Now it was a typewriter given with such
graceful sweetness to a literary worker whose
sight was failing; now checks that saved the

day for one or another; again the numerous
subscriptions to worthy objects; or the countless gifts and helps to friends. A woman
lecturer had been ill and unfortunate, but
had several modest engagements waiting in a
neighboring city if only she had ten dollars
to get there. Mrs. Moulton sent her fifty
that she might have a margin for comforts
that she needed. To a friend in want of
aid to bridge over a short time was sent a
check, totally unsolicited and undreamed of,
and accepted as a loan; but when the recipient had, soon afterward, a birthday, a delicate
note from Mrs. Moulton made the supposed
loan a birthday gift. Never did any one make
such a fine art of giving as did she. Pages
could be filled with these instances — the complete list, indeed, is known to the Recording
Angel only.

All the world of letters was talked over in
those morning hours in her room. Sometimes
her friends "gently wrangled," and bantered
her with laughter and love. At one time she
had made in a lyric a familiar allusion to
larks and nightingales, and Louise Guiney,
who, because she bore Mrs. Moulton's name,
usually addressed her as " Godmam," took
her to task for some ornithological inad-
vertence in the terrestrial location of her

nightingale. Colonel Higginson, in a review of her poems, had quoted the stanza:

> Shall I lie down to sleep, and see no more
> The splendid affluence of earth and sky?
> The morning lark to the far heavens soar,
> The nightingale with the soft dusk draw nigh?

and had ungallantly commented:

"But Mrs. Moulton has lain down to sleep all her life in America, and never looked forward to seeing the morning lark on awakening. She never saw or sought the nightingale at dusk in the green lanes of her native Connecticut. Why should she revert to the habits of her colonial ancestors, and meditate on these pleasing foreign fowl as necessary stage-properties for a vision of death and immortality?"

Another writer had come to the defence of the poet in this fashion:

"Considering that Mrs. Moulton goes to Europe the last of every April, not returning till late in October, it would seem natural for her to sing of 'larks and nightingales,' since she must hear them both sing in the English May. Do, dear Colonel Higginson, permit her to sing of them, though they are not native birds, since in the magic of her art she almost makes us hear them too."

Miss Guiney, laughing over these comments, turned to Mrs. Moulton.

"Godmam," she asked, "did you ever see a nightingale?"

"Why, yes, Louise; plenty of them."

"Where?"

"Why, anywhere. Out here, I suppose," replied the elder poet, dreamily glancing from the windows of her morning-room into the tree-tops of Rutland Square. "In London, too, I believe," she added, rather vaguely.

"Singing in Trafalgar Square, godmam," rejoined the younger poet mischievously.

The informal loiterers in the morning-room were never weary of asking Mrs. Moulton's impressions of London writers.

"You knew Thomas Hardy well?" someone would ask.

"I knew him. I even venture to think of him as a friend — at least as a very friendly acquaintance. I cared deeply for many of his books before I had the pleasure of meeting him; and I quite adored 'The Return of the Native.'"

"And you liked the author as well as the books?"

"I think no one could know Thomas Hardy and not like him. He is sympathetic, genial, unaffected, altogether delightful; somewhat pessimistic, to be sure, and with a vein of sadness — a minor chord in his psalm of life: but all the same with a keen sense of fun. I remember I was telling him once about an American admirer of his. It was at a party at Hardy's own house, and a few people were listening to our talk. The American of whose praise I spoke was Charles T. Copeland, of Harvard, who had just reviewed 'Tess,' in the *Atlantic Monthly*. Mr. Hardy listened kindly, and then he said, 'What you say is a consolation, just now.' I knew some good fun lurked behind the quaint humor of his smile. 'Why just now?' I asked. 'Oh, I dined, two nights ago, at the house of a Member of Parliament. It was by way of being a political dinner; but, as "Tess" was just out, one and another spoke of it — kindly enough. Finally one lady, two or three seats away from me, leaned forward. Her clear voice commanded every one's attention. "Well, Mr. Hardy," she said, "these people are complaining that you had Tess hanged in the last chapter of your book. *That* is not what I complain of. I complain because you did not have all your characters hanged, for they all deserved it!" Don't you think, Mrs. Moulton, that after that I need consolation from somewhere?'"

Many of her reminiscences which entered into the talk have been told in her newspaper letters, and need not be repeated here, but they took on a fresh vitality from the living voice and the gracious, unaffected manner.

By some untraced or unanalyzed impulse Mrs. Moulton was apt to be moved on each New Year's day to write a poem. Usually this was a sonnet, but now and then a lyric instead; and for many years the first entry in the fresh volume of her diary records the fact. On the first of January, 1890, she writes:

"Began the New Year by writing a sonnet, to be called 'How Shall We Know,' unless I can find a better title."

"The Last Good-bye" was the title upon which she afterward fixed.

On the fifth day of January of this year died Dr. Westland Marston. Mrs. Moulton wrote in her *Herald* letters a review of his life and work, in the course of which she said with touching earnestness:

"I scarcely know a life which has been so tragic as his in the way of successive bereavements; and when I think of him as I saw him last, on the first day of last November — in his solitary library, with the pictures of those he had loved and lost on its walls, and with only their ghosts for his daily company — I almost feel that, for his own sake, I ought to be glad that he has gone to join the beloved ones whom one can easily fancy making festival of welcome for him."

Her intimacy had been close with all the family, and while Edmund Gosse was right when he wrote to her that she seemed to him always to have been "Philip's true guardian-ray, or better genius," her friendship for Cecily Marston, for Mrs. O'Shaughnessy, and with Dr. Marston himself was hardly less close. The tragic ending of the family could not but cast a bleak shade over the opening year.

Her relations with English writers and the good offices by which she helped to make their work better known on this side of the Atlantic might be illustrated by numerous letters.

Richard Garnett to Mrs. Moulton

BRITISH MUSEUM, LONDON,
August 4, 1890.

DEAR MRS. MOULTON: I hope I need not say how your letter has gratified me. The progress of "The Twilight of the Gods" has been slow, and I was especially disappointed that the endeavor to introduce it to the American public through an American publisher fell through. But there seems token of its gradually making way, and I value your approbation among the most signal. I shall be delighted to receive the copy of your poems, which I know I can safely promise to admire.

Believe me,

Most sincerely yours,

R. GARNETT.

Both Edmund Clarence Stedman and George Meredith had, each unknown to the other, suggested to Mrs. Moulton that she write a novel in verse. "Lucile" and "Aurora Leigh" had each in its time and way made a wide popular success, and they felt that Mrs. Moulton might succeed equally. To this suggestion Mr. Meredith alludes in a letter in which he thanks Mrs. Moulton for a copy of "In the Garden of Dreams."

George Meredith to Mrs. Moulton

MARCH 9, 1890.

"DEAR MRS MOULTON: Your beautiful little volume charms us all. It is worth a bower of song, and I am rightly sensible of the gift. You are getting to a mastery of the sonnet that is rare, and the lyrics are exquisite. I hope you will now be taking some substantial theme, a narrative, for ampler exercise of your powers. I am hard at work and nearing the end of a work that has held me for some time. I have not been in London since the day of Browning's funeral, — a sad one, but having its glory. I had a tinge of apprehension the other day in hearing of Russell Lowell's illness. We have been reassured about him. Boston, I suppose, will soon be losing you. . . ."

In the years directly following its publication, "In the Garden of Dreams" went rapidly through several editions. One sonnet which elicited much praise was that called

HELP THOU MINE UNBELIEF.

Because I seek Thee not, oh seek Thou me!
  Because my lips are dumb, oh hear the cry
  I do not utter as Thou passest by
And from my life-long bondage set me free!
Because, content, I perish far from Thee,
  Oh, seize me, snatch me from my fate, and try
  My soul in Thy consuming fire! Draw nigh
And let me, blinded, Thy salvation see.
If I were pouring at Thy feet my tears,
  If I were clamoring to see Thy face,
I should not need Thee, Lord, as now I need,
Whose dumb, dead soul knows neither hopes nor fears,
  Nor dreads the outer darkness of this place —
Because I seek not, pray not, give Thou heed!

The deeply religious feeling, the profound sincerity, and what might perhaps not inaptly be called the completely modern mood of this, a mood which in its essence is permanent but which in its outward form varies with each generation, gave it a power of wide appeal. A church paper in England said of it:

"Profound faith in the infinite goodness of God is the spirit which animates most of Mrs. Moulton's work. The sonnet . . . deserves a place among the best devotional verse in the language. It is a question if, outside of the volume of Miss Rossetti, any devotional verse to equal this can be found in the work of a living woman-writer."

The critic need hardly have limited himself to the poetry of women. Mrs. Moulton was all her life vitally interested in the religious side of life, and many more of her letters might have been quoted to show how constantly her mind returned to the question of immortality and human responsibility. The sonnet had become for her a natural mode of utterance, as it was for Mrs. Browning when she wrote the magnificent sequence which recorded her love; and in this especial poem is the essence of Mrs. Moulton's spiritual life.

Mrs. Moulton's mastery of the sonnet has been alluded to before, but as each new volume brought fresh proof of it, and as she went on producing work equally important, it is impossible not to refer to this form of her art again and again. Whittier wrote to her after the appearance of "In the Garden of Dreams": "It seems to me the sonnet was never set to such music before, nor ever weighted with more deep and tender thought;" and Miss Guiney, in a review, declared that "we rest with a steadfast pleasure on the sonnets, and in their masterly handling of high thoughts." Phrases of equal significance might be multiplied, and to them no dissenting voice could be raised.

In 1890 Mrs. Moulton brought out a volume of juvenile stories under the title "Stories Told at Twilight," and in 1896 this was followed by another with the name "In Childhood's Country." Always wholesome, kindly, attractive, these volumes had a marked success with the audience for which they were designed; and of few books written for children can or need more be said.

Among the letters of this period are a number from a correspondent signing "Pascal Germain." The writer had published a novel called "Rhea: a Suggestion," but his identity

has not yet been made public.   Mrs. Moulton
never knew who he was, but apparently opened
the correspondence in regard to something
which struck her in the book.   Some clews
exist which might be followed up were one
inclined to endeavor to solve the riddle.
After the death of Carl Gutherz, the artist
who painted the admirable decoration "Light"
for the ceiling of the Reading-room in the
Congressional Library in Washington, his
daughter found among the papers of her
father a post-card signed Pascal Germain,
and written from Paris in the manner of a
familiar friend.   Evidently Mr. Gutherz had
known the mysterious writer well, but the
daughter had no clew by which to identify
him.

A letter from Edward Stanton Huntington,
author of "Dreams of the Dead," rather
deepens than clears the mystery.   The writer
was a nephew of Bishop Huntington, and is
not now living.

Mr. Huntington to Mrs. Moulton

"WOLLASTON, MASS.
December 8, 1892.

" MY DEAR MRS. MOULTON: I find myself
unable to send the complete letters of my
friend, Duynsters, but take pleasure in sending

you the extracts referring to Pascal Germain. After the receipt of his letter (enclosed) dated June 1st, I wrote him of the conversation you and I had in regard to 'Rhea' and the merits of the book. I also mentioned the photograph. He replies:

" 'What you tell me of the photograph and Mrs. Moulton amuses me very much. Let me assure you that the photograph is no more the picture of Pascal Germain than it is of Pericles, or Gaboriau, or Zoroaster. I am the only human being who knows the identity of Germain, beside himself, and no one can possess his photograph.'

"Duynsters then goes on to discuss the symbolism and sound psychology of the work. My own conclusion, after reading the words of my friend Duynsters, and hastily perusing 'Rhea,' (I confess I was not much interested in the book) — my conclusions are that Germain is the pen name of some man or woman of peculiar genius and eccentric taste.

"Mr. Duynsters is a very cultivated man, one who has travelled extensively, and who has a keen judgment of men and affairs; so it puzzles me exceedingly to decide who this author of 'Rhea' really is. Time will tell. . . ."

A copy of "Rhea" was among Mrs. Moulton's books, but the novel seems never to have made a marked impression on either side of the Atlantic. What is apparently the earliest letter remaining of the series seems to throw light on a passage in the note of Mr. Huntington, and to give the impression that Pascal Germain had played a mischievous trick on Mrs. Moulton by sending her a photograph which was not genuine.

M. Germain to Mrs. Moulton

MONASTERY OF STE. BARBE,
SEINE INFÉRIEURE, FRANCE.

MADAME: It is in sincere gratitude that I tender you my thanks for your kind words about the photograph which I had many misgivings in venturing to lay before you, fearing it might be *de trop*. Whether you really forgive me for sending it, or were so gentle as to conceal your displeasure, it leaves me your debtor always. Although I write from Paris now, the above is my address, and I beg you will remember it if at any time I can serve you on this side of the ocean. I beg you to command me freely.

Believe me to remain,
Yours very faithfully,
PASCAL GERMAIN.

From the same

PARIS. Tuesday Morn.

DEAR FRIEND: I am inexpressibly touched by your letter, and I reply at once. I drop all other work to write to you, solely that I may lose no time. Yours of the 1st has been here only a few minutes. Believe me, your idea of death is purely a fancy, born of an atmosphere of doubt, out of which you must get as soon as possible. I am glad you wrote, for in this I may serve you as I have served others.

When I tell you I feel sure your phantom of approaching death is unreal, I am telling you a truth deduced from hard study, and than which no other conclusion could arrive. Of this I give you my most sacred assurance. Put this thought out of your mind as you would recoil from any adverse suggestion. The fact is, very few deaths are natural: they are the result of fear. The natural death is at the age of from a hundred to a hundred and twenty or thirty years. The deaths about us are from fright, ignorance, and concession to the opinions of uneducated friends, and half-educated doctors. This I know. I could cite you case after case of those who have really died because the physician asserted they could not live.

If your delusion is mental, swing to the other side of the circle, and read or study the most agreeable things that are widely apart from what you have been dwelling upon. Exercise strengthens the mind. It is the folly of fools to speak of the brain being over-worked. It may be stupidly exercised, but if used in a catholic development, the use makes it more vigorous. Look at the blue sky; not the ground. God is the Creator, but man is also a creator. His health depends largely on his will, — that is to say, in the sense of that will being plastic to the Divine will.

If your illness is physical stop thinking about yourself, — do as Saint Teresa did, take up some other subject, and suddenly you will find yourself well. Nature requires only a few months, not years, to make the body all over again.

Death is natural. Few physicians know anything about it. They have shut down every window in their souls to the light. For your comfort let me tell you that what I am saying is the subject of a long talk with one of the first physicians on the Continent.

Many things, accepted by the common

people to be the result of miracle, are really
the result of thought. That is, of mental force,
used or misused. Don't misuse your forces.
Read Plato if you have been reading too much
modern fiction, or have been dipping too deep
into Wittemberg's philosophy. It seems to
me there can be no doubt of the survival of the
individual soul. Why not plant your feet on
the facts we possess, and on faith, and philosophy? Read your "Imitatione Christi." It
fits every mind by transposing the symbolism.
I tell you frankly that even if no such man as
Jesus ever lived, I can be serene with Plato's
guidance and light.

Stop critical reading. Really a critic is an
interpreter, but what modern critic knows
this? The only modern critic I honor is
Herbert Spencer.

Believe me,
Yours with great respect,
PASCAL GERMAIN.

From the same

17, AVENUE GOURGARD (MONCEAU), PARIS,
September 13, 1890.

MY DEAR MRS. MOULTON: I hope you have
believed that all this while I have been away
my letters were not forwarded and only now

can I thank you for the beautiful volume you
have sent me.

I have wandered through it reading over
and over special poems that fascinate me. I
have not really read them all yet, though I
ought to know this volume very well, for
I bought it some years ago. I am particularly
pleased with the poems, "A Painted Fan,"
and "The House of Death." The poem
called "Annie's Daughter" is picturesque to
a great degree. By the way I have a letter
from an American magazine asking me to
write for them "anything." The letter is in
French. Now why should I not write for them
an article on your poems? They tell me they
will faithfully translate all I send. Your in-
formant was right. I am French only on one
side of the house. Lest I may forget, I want
to say here and now how much I like your "At
Étretat." I should have known it meant that
place, even without the title. The picture is
so vivid. Do you know the Riviera? There
is material for you in grays and browns, and
the sound of the sea. But I think the poetry
of the "fan" expresses you best, and there you
have the advantage of being alone in your
beautiful thought. What lonely things beauty,
truth, and the soul are! The atoms never
touch.

Forgive the length of this if you can, and
believe me,

>Your faithful servant,
>>PASCAL GERMAIN.

From the same

17, AVENUE GOURGARD (MONCEAU), PARIS,
December 24, 1891.

MADAME: I trust it will not displease you
to hear from me again, though my fate is
perilously uncertain, since not from you, nor
from any mutual friend, can I be sure that my
"Rhea" has not fallen under your displeasure.
But I offer something more welcome to your
poet's hands than any work of mine. The
laurel which I enclose is from the casket of
dear Owen Meredith. You may have seen in
the newspapers an account of the brilliantly
solemn funeral, when honors were paid him
which only before have been paid to the Chief
Marshals of France; and how through all
that pomp and pageantry, but one laurel
wreath rested on his casket, — the crown laid
upon his beloved clay by his wife.

There was a good deal of talk about this
wreath, though no one but Lady Lytton and
the sender knew from whence it came. It
was I — yet not altogether myself, — for it
was a late (too late) atonement for an unde-

livered message of love and thanks to the
author of "Lucile" sent to him by a dear
friend of mine, a Sister of Charity.

Lord Lytton's death was, as you know, sudden, and my message was unwritten because I
had only returned to Paris after years of
travelling, and I was simply waiting for better news of him in order to go to the Embassy
with the story of her life, and what the ideal
woman in the poem had done for the heroine
in the flesh, when the startling news of his
death came. I did what I thought the dear
Sister would like done, since words were useless. One might quote his own words,

Soul to soul,

since from my hands to the poet's wife the
laurel was laid upon him; and I send it because it has a touch of the supernatural; of
the mystical love and sweetness of your own
domain, — and is no common occurrence, that,
out of all the wreaths and tokens, sent by
kings and queens and nobles, from all over
the world, the one alone from a Sister of
Charity, was laid upon his casket from the
first, in the death-chamber, in the church,
and in the sad procession, and finally buried
with him at Knebworth. For I must explain that not till a fortnight afterward did

Lady Lytton know that the laurel crown was not my gift alone. It was purely as my gift that she generously favored it above all others.

She was profoundly touched when I told her the story, and only last Sunday she wrote and asked me if she might some day give it to the public, to which, of course, I assented. I am therefore breaking no confidence in sending these few leaves which I plucked from the wreath after it was woven. As they had faded I regilded them, as you see. (Laurels and gold for poets.) Nor is this boldness all mine. It is my artist friend, Monsieur Carl Gutherz, who bids me send them to you, "because," he says, "they will weave into her fancies in some sweet and satisfying dream."

Madame, believe me,

Your faithful servant,

PASCAL GERMAIN.

Among the Moulton books now in the collection in the Boston Public Library is a 16mo copy of Bernardin de Saint-Pierre's "Paul et Virginie," bound in an old brocade of a lovely hue of old-rose. On its cover obliquely is to be seen the faintest shadow of a cross, and in it is preserved the following letter:

M. Germain to Mrs. Moulton

Paris, Wednesday.

MY DEAR MRS. MOULTON: The little book is not *quite* what I was looking for. The binding I was searching for I did not find, but if I delay too long, I shall be away to Madrid; *not* the place most likely to reward my search.

I wonder if you will like the odd cover? It was ordered by me in an impulse without stopping to reflect that its associations to me mean nothing to you. The bit of tapestry is the relic of one of the oldest and most picturesque chambers in Normandy, and was given me by a nun who nursed me through an illness there — in fact I begged her for it because it is interwoven with a story which I think my best (not yet finished). If you hold the book so that the light plays horizontally, you will see the trace of time-wear in the shape of a †. The fabric was the vestment more than a hundred years in the service of the church there, and was worn by the hero of my story — a priest whose life was a long agony — for a fault nobly atoned. But I must not assume your interest in the tragedy. Perhaps the color — which an artist friend borrowed to robe one of his angels in — may please you. If not, kindly burn the packet, as it has been consecrated — the fabric, not the book; — for I owe the giver the courtesy of conforming to the old Catholic (nay, Egyptian, for the matter of that) rule to burn all sacred things when their day is done.

No doubt the cover does not look professional. I got it done at short notice by one not used to my sometimes eccentric requests and wishes. Will you kindly give it value by accepting it with the best wishes of

Your very faithful,

PASCAL GERMAIN.

So these letters remain, with their curious suggestiveness.

Mrs. Moulton's memorial volume on Arthur O'Shaughnessy was published in 1894, — a volume containing selections from his poems preceded by a biographical and critical introduction. Mrs. Spofford pronounced the book "an exquisite piece of work, full of interest and done with such delight in touch." Mrs. Moulton had written with her accustomed skill, and through every line spoke her intimate sympathy with the poet and with his work.

Her summers, after the visit to her daughter in Charleston, were still passed in Europe. Rome, Florence, and other southern cities were often visited before she went to England for her annual London season. Often, too, she made a stay in Paris either before or after her sojourn on the other side of the Channel. Among her friends in Paris were Marie Bashkirtseff and her mother, and not infrequently she took tea at the studio. After the death of the artist, a number of letters passed between Mrs. Moulton and the heart-broken mother.

Her friends in London were so many, and the diary records so many pleasant social diversions that it is no wonder that Thomas Hardy should write to her: "Why don't you live in London altogether? You might thus please us, your friends, and send to America letters of a higher character than are usually penned. You would raise the standard of that branch of journalism." Season after season she notes dinners, luncheons, drives, functions of all sorts, and one does not wonder that with this and her really arduous literary work her health began to suffer. A German "cure" came to be a regular part of the summer programme, and yet with her eager temperament and keen interest in the human, she could not bring herself to forego the excitement and enjoyment which probably did much to make this necessary.

Not a little did her voluminous correspondence add to the strain under which she lived. Continually in her diary are entries which show how heavy was the task of keeping up with the flood of correspondence which constantly flowed in at her doors. "Letters, letters, letters to answer. Oh, dear, it seems to me that the whole of my life goes in writing letters. I wrote what seemed necessary letters till one P. M. Oh, what shall I do? These letters are ruining my life!" "Letters *all* the morning." "Letters till luncheon." Her acquaintance was wide, and her relations with the literary world of her day made it inevitable that she should be called upon for large epistolary labors; but added to this was the burden, already alluded to, of the letters which came to her from strangers. She was too kindly to ignore or neglect these, and she expended much of her strength in answer to calls upon her which were unwarrantably made. Against the greater amount of literary work which she might have accomplished with the force thus generously expended, or the possible days which might have been added to her life, must in the great account be set the pleasure she gave to many, and the balance is not for man to reckon.

It is now well known that the poems published over the name "Michael Field" were

written by Miss Bradley and Miss Edith
Cooper in conjunction. To Miss Cooper,
Mrs. Moulton, in the intimacy of a warm
friendship which established itself between
them, gave in loving familiarity the name
"Amber Eyes." Many letters were exchanged,
and from the correspondence of Miss Cooper
may be quoted these fragments.

Miss Cooper to Mrs. Moulton

"We have just returned from Fiesole and
Orvieto, and such names are poems. I had
hoped to send you verses in *The Academy*,
welded by Michael, on some Greek goddess
in the British Museum. We very much care
for the sympathy and interest of Americans."

"I don't know any poet who is so spontaneously true to himself as you are. I actually
stand by you as I read, and see the harmonious movement of your lips, and the half-
deprecating, half-shadowed look in your eyes.
. . . Your verses are like music. What is
this? You are not able to sing? Is this the
effect of Boston on its winter guest? I can
sympathize, for I have not written a line since
our play was brought out last October."

"The placid hills [in the Lake Country]
make one love them as only Tuscan hills be-

sides can do. Some of the greatest ballads belong here. Wordsworth, Scott, and Burns, and many song-writers have given their passion to this country-side, where one has such joy as the best dreams are made of."

"In a cover somewhat like this paper in tone 'Stéphanie' presents herself to you. . . . We have the audacity to think it is nearly as well woven as one of the William Morris carpets. We have taken ten years over the ten pages."

On one of her visits to the cure at Wiesbaden Mrs. Moulton made the acquaintance of Friedrich von Bodenstedt and visited at his house. She characterized the lyrics of the author of the "Lieder des Mirza-Schaffy" as "warm with the love of life and the life of love, and perfumed with the roses of the East." Her description of his personal appearance is not without interest.

"A tall, handsome, active man of seventy-two, with gray hair, with eyes full, still, of the keen fire of youth; with the grand manner which belongs to the high-bred gentlemen of his generation, and the gift to please and to charm which is not always the dower even of a poet."

Her return voyage from Europe in 1891 was a sorrowful one. Just before sailing she notes in

LOUISA REBECCA CHANDLER, MRS. MOULTON'S MOTHER

Page 199

her diary: "A sad day, — a telegram in the morning to say that mother was failing." On the day before the steamer made land she writes: "A lovely day, but I am so anxious as to what news of my poor mother awaits me to-morrow"; and the first entry on shore is: "Landed to learn that my dear mother died last Monday, October 26, and was buried Tuesday. Oh, what it is to know that I shall never see her again!"

The letters of Mrs. Moulton show through these years a growing feeling in regard to the mystery of death. So many of her friends had gone that the brevity of life was more and more deeply impressed upon her. In the correspondence of many of her friends are traces that her letters to them, not now available, had touched upon the questions to her so vital. Mrs. Maxwell (Miss M. E. Braddon) for instance, wrote:

Mrs. Maxwell to Mrs. Moulton

"I have never believed in the gloomy and pitiless creed of the Calvinists. I believe every one is master of his destiny so far as perfect freedom of choice for good or evil. When we take the wrong road we do it perhaps in the blindness of passion, with eyes blind to consequences, minds darkened by selfish desires, by vanity, false ambitions, and by weakly yielding to bad influences."

Canon Bell to Mrs. Moulton

"I hope you are seeing your way clearly to faith in God and His dear Son. A sure trust in our Heavenly Father is the only true consolation in this world of change and sorrow. That brings peace."

Lady Henry Somerset to Mrs. Moulton

"I well understand what you say about looking onward. I think our eyes are turned that way when the steps of life lead us nearer to the journey's end with each setting sun. It is absorbingly interesting. Yes, I believe the love of God will be closest; and, in the last, victorious."

What the words were to which these were replies may in part be gathered from the following:

Mrs. Moulton to William Winter

DURNHAM HOUSE, CHELSEA, LONDON,
October 3, 1894.

DEAR WILLIE: I hope your lecture last night was a success, but it seems to me that all you do is. Yes, — how well I remember that seventieth-birthday breakfast to Dr.

Holmes. We sat very near each other, you and I, and I know how your words moved me, as well as how they moved Dr. Holmes. I felt his death very keenly, but I knew him far less than you did. To know him at all was to love him. How strange that you should have written of so many great pilgrims into the unknown. Thank God for your immortal hope. To me the outlook darkens as I draw nearer and nearer to the end. I am appalled by the immensity of the universe, and the nothingness of our little human atom among the infinite worlds. But God knows what is to come. You are happier than most in the love that surrounds you.

Thank you a thousand times for your dear letter. If I go to New York or you come to Boston, do not let us fail to meet, for the time in which earthly meetings are possible is short. Oh, how I hope there may be a life to come in which we shall find lost loves and hopes, and above all, lost possibilities. I think it is hardest of all to me to think what I might have been, might have done, and to be so utterly discontented with myself as I am. If you pray, say a prayer sometimes for one of the truest and fondest of your many friends, — this wanderer,

L. C. M.

Without doubt the state of Mrs. Moulton's health had much to do with her apprehensions in regard to a future life, and no one who was intimately associated with her could fail to know that these expressions of gloom and foreboding, while entirely genuine at the moment of their utterance, convey an impression of her usual state of mind far more dark than was warranted by the truth. She was too sincerely interested in life and friendship, too much of her time and thought went to earnest work, however, for her to be in general either brooding or fearsome. The extracts given rather indicate her attitude of mind toward certain grave questions than toward life in general.

The frankness of the following letter from a woman who possessed remarkable powers which the public never fully appreciated is striking and refreshing:

Mrs. Richard Henry Stoddard to Mrs. Moulton

MATTAPOISETT, January 20.

DEAR MRS. MOULTON: Will you accept Mr. Stoddard's thanks for your pleasant notice through me? I write nearly all his personal letters, I may say, nearly all except business letters. He was always averse to letter writing, and since his blindness this aversion is increased; he hurts and angers many without meaning to do so.

I think your first quotation a very poor one. The value of reviews or notices seems to me to be in quotations rather than in the ordinary criticism. In reading them I have often taken the poems in a new and striking light; the medium — that is, the writer — has instructed and cleared my understanding. The happiest in regard to "The Lion's Cub" is the extract in *The Critic*. There has been no review of the book; the nearest, so far, is the *Springfield Republican's* and that is suggestive of a review. Mr. Stoddard considers the book a failure; I doubt if he ever collects again. Boyle O'Reilly once said that he saw Stoddard in Broadway and that no one noticed him; "had he been in Boston," he continued, "on Washington Street, every man's hat would have been off to his white head."

We are most delightfully set aside from the afternoon teas of the city, though the invitations chase us up here; the gray tranquil waters of our little bay, the solitary street, a dog occasionally going by, sometimes a man, is a pleasing contrast to 15th Street and Broadway. We shall remain a few days longer and then go into our incongruous life again. If Lorimer were acting in Boston as he did for the past three winters, we should go home that way, but as he has not been there this season we shall not appear.

Have you come across my friend, young Edward McDowell, the composer, who has made such a success? He and his wife are charming.

And Miss ——, will you give her my regards when you see her? She has been not only attentive to me, but to my young sister, who followeth not in her aged sister's steps.

Mr. Stoddard also wished to be remembered kindly to you.

Yours truly,
ELIZABETH STODDARD.

P. S. I meant to say while on "The Lion's Cub" that I never was so impressed with the gravity and dignity of S.'s verse, nor so clearly saw the profound melancholy of his mind. He really cares little for life. Ah, me!

E. S.

CHAPTER VII

1895–1900

. . . The laurel and the praise
But unto them, true helpers of their kind,
Who, daily walking by imagined streams
Rear fanes empyreal in Verse of Gold, —
Rare architects of figments and of dreams. — LLOYD MIFFLIN.

That jar of violet wine set in the air,
That palest rose sweet in the night of life.
—STEPHEN PHILLIPS.

I give you a day of my life;
My uttermost gift and my best. — L. C. M.

THE last decade of the century, to half of which the preceding chapter was given, stands out pre-eminently in Mrs. Moulton's life. Her fame, which had come to her so untainted by any self-seeking, and the abounding richness of friendship which so filled her life, friendship as sympathetic and cordial as it was widespread, made these years wonderful. Death and sorrow did bring into them a profound sadness, but even these brought her into closer touch with humanity and ripened her experiences. The recognition which her art won gave her something much more satisfying than merely

. . . to hear the nations praising her far off.

And if to deal with literature is only to know
about the Eternal Beauty, while living and
loving are in it and of it, she was indeed fortunate. In the life of no poet could be less of the
abstraction of literary fame and more of the
vitality of real existence. Her social life, both
at home and abroad, was full of companionship sweet and genuine. For the mere cere-
monial of life she cared little. Life was to her
a thing too real, too precious, to make of it a
spectacle. If her association was so largely
with persons of distinction, it was because they
interested her personally, and not because of
the social position. That was incidental.
Mrs. Kate Gannett Wells, speaking after the
death of Mrs. Moulton, remarked: "I honored her for her literary power; I loved her
for herself. But especially I felt her refinement." Such refinement is incompatible with
ostentation, and it was significant of her feeling on social matters that she copied in her
note-book, with the remark, "I agree with
this entirely," this paragraph from Henry
James' "Siege of London":

"I hate that phrase 'getting into society.'
I don't think one ought to attribute to one's
self that sort of ambition. One ought to
assume that one is in society — that one is

society — and to hold that if one has good manners, one has from the social point of view achieved the great thing. The rest regards others."

While she was a woman of the world, she was not a worldly woman. She might easily have been presented at court during her many seasons in London, but she never cared to be. She not infrequently met the Princess Louise and other members of the Royal Family, and her own comings and goings were chronicled in the London press. She was the guest and the intimate friend of titled persons in England and of those first in American society; but all this never altered her simple and utterly unaffected cordiality toward those who were of no social prominence whatever. "The reason for her popularity," wrote Miss Josephine Jenkins very justly, "is summed up in the sympathy of her nature, which expands with loving and often helpful solicitude to those seeking encouragement, precisely as it expands toward those having attained some noble distinction. Not every human being is endowed with this genius for appreciation."

Mrs. Moulton wrote to Coulson Kernahan on one occasion: "I do wonder who spoke of me as 'a woman, above all things, of society.'

Nothing could be more remote from truth. I simply will not go to balls; I don't care for large receptions, though I do go to them sometimes; I enjoy dinners, if I am by the right person. But I refuse ten invitations to every one I accept, and the thing I most and really care for in all the world is the love of congenial friends and quiet, intimate tête-à-tête with them. The superficial, external side of life is nothing to me. I long for honest and true love as a child set down in a desert might long for the mother's sheltering arms."

On New Year's day, 1895, she wrote, with that curious periodicity which characterized the opening of so many years for her, a sonnet entitled "Oh, Traveller by Unaccustomed Ways," fine and strong, and with haunting lines such as:

> Searcher among new worlds for pleasures new. — ...
> Some wild, sweet fragrance of remembered days.

The sestet is as follows:

> I send my message to thee by the stars —
>   Since other messenger I may not find
> Till I go forth beyond these prisoning bars,
>   Leaving this memory-haunted world behind,
> To seek thee, claim thee, wheresoe'er thou be,
> Since Heaven itself were empty, lacking thee.

The letters of this time are as usual full of allusions to Mrs. Moulton's work, and are as usual from a very wide circle of literary friends. Sir Frederick Pollock expresses his appreciation of her book upon Marston, and the pleasure he and Lady Pollock anticipate in seeing her in London next season. J. T. Trowbridge writes to her that the technique of her songs and sonnets "is well-nigh faultless, and their melody never fails to respond to the tender feeling by which they are inspired." Lord de Tabley thanks her for a notice of his work, "and particularly," he adds, "for putting me in such good company as that of William Watson, whom I greatly admire." Sir Lewis Morris writes cordially, and reminds her of their "pleasant lunches at Lord Haylston's." Marie Corelli expresses her gratitude for pleasant things which Mrs. Moulton has said of her in a letter to Mrs. Coulson Kernahan. Other letters were from Miss Bayley (Edna Lyall), Andrew Lang, Rose Kingsley, Lady Temple, Stephen Phillips, the Hon. Florence Henniker. If, as Emerson says, "a letter is a spiritual gift," these gifts were showered upon Mrs. Moulton.

William Watson to Mrs. Moulton

DEAR MRS. MOULTON: One of the most generous recognitions of my early poems came from your pen. I wished then to express my

14

gratitude. I look forward to the pleasure of making your acquaintance. I am touched by your kind sympathy, and I know that you gladden all our group of friends. It is no ordinary thanks I owe you for your generous and delightful criticism. I have to thank you, already, for my best appreciation in America. You do not know how grateful I am to the first woman in America (and almost the first human being) who gave me hearty and inspiring praise. Your poems add to my store of beautiful things, and I do not prize them the less because some of their qualities are my own despair. When your letter came, that article which I call my conscience, and which I wear less for use than for ornament, gave me no peace. Yet the outward parts of life were to blame rather than I, their victim. I had been moving, and giving the Post Office the trouble of one who inherits a wandering tendency. I hope you will permit me to call upon you when next you are in London, and I am, dear Mrs. Moulton,

Sincerely yours,

WILLIAM WATSON.

To a friend Mr. Watson wrote of Mrs. Moulton: "Her letters show her absolute goodness of heart, which is worth all other human qualities put together."

Mrs. Frances Hodgson Burnett writes characteristically of that inner inspirer which she calls her "Fairy."

Mrs. Burnett to Mrs. Moulton

". . . I am so glad you like my story. . . . It was not I who said 'Human beings can do anything if they set their minds to it'; it was that beloved thing which has said things for me all my life. Sometimes I call it 'The Fairy,' but I think it must be a kind of splendid spirit. It is so strong, it is so good to me, and I do so love it. When I said that thing it seemed to make something waken within me. I began to say it to myself, and to believe it. Only thus could I have finished the story, and this makes me know it is true. . . . I have sometimes thought the thing I had to give is nearly always part of a story, some note of love, or message that rings clear. I don't ask it should be a loud note, only that some one shall hear it and remember. The fact that you have heard, makes the story a success, so far as I am concerned. As for giving, you give always. I have seen that. You give of gentleness and kindness and all things that help. Your hands are full of things to give."

Just before Mrs. Moulton's sailing in the spring of 1895 a breakfast was given to her by a group of her friends, at which the decoration was very prettily all of mountain laurel. In the centre of the table was a basket of green osiers filled with the faintly pink kalmia, and this color-scheme was carried out in the menu-cards, the embroidered centre-piece, the candle-shades, and in the Venetian glass with which the table was furnished. It is to this breakfast that Mrs. Blake alludes in the little note which follows:

Mrs. John G. Blake to Mrs. Moulton

DEAR MRS. MOULTON: Among all the laurels which are being laid before your conquering feet, will you take my little flower of good-will and congratulations? The sonnets are exquisite, so are you always to

Your affectionate

M. E. B.

In 1896 was published "Lazy Tours," Mrs. Moulton's most important book in prose. This volume records her impressions in her wanderings in Spain, in Southern Italy, in France, and in Switzerland. It is a delightful mosaic of bits about people and places, of glimpses of Rome, of Florence, of Paris, of the German "cures," and of pleasant experiences of all sorts. The book is dedicated to Sir

Bruce and Lady Seton, "The well-beloved friends and frequent hosts of this lazy tourist." The dedication is as appropriate as it is pleasantly phrased, for the Setons were not only among the closest of Mrs. Moulton's English friends, but with them she had done a great deal of journeying. The book is charmingly vivid, and is a pleasant companion for the traveller in the places with which it deals. Mrs. Moulton neither was nor claimed to be an expert critic of painting and sculpture, but her artistic taste responded sensitively to what was best, and she recorded her feelings with a frank enthusiasm and a wonderful freshness.

Arlo Bates, in acknowledging a gift copy of "Lazy Tours" wrote: "I thank you for 'Lazy Tours.' It is done with a touch not only light and delicate, but strangely gentle. It is written with the experience of a woman and the enthusiasm of a girl." In another note of Mr. Bates', belonging to this time, are the remarks:

"Friendship is about the only real thing in humanity."

"The few of us who, in this muse-forgotten age, still care for real poetry, are to be congratulated no less."

The sculptor Greenough wrote: "Verily, your 'Lazy Tours' are a rebuke to industry, for it has woven a magic carpet, as that of the 'Arabian Nights,' only you transport the reader, in every sense of the word. . . . What excellent prose you poets write when you try." The critics were all agreed, and the verdict of the public endorsed that of Mrs. Moulton's friends and of the reviewers. The book had precisely that lightness of touch which is perennially charming, and which perhaps is due equally to literary expertness and to innate good taste.

The usual summer abroad, full of social experiences, followed; and then the winter in Boston with the crowded Friday receptions. A letter which belongs to this winter is full of a lightness and kindliness characteristic of the writer.

James Whitcomb Riley to Mrs. Moulton

". . . You, after months and months of barbarous silence, are asking me why I have not written! Well, I 'll answer in my artlessness and most truthfully tell you that my last letter (and a really appealing one) meeting with no response whatever, I just had concluded that I 'd win highest favor in your estimate by not writing. So I quit writing, and

WILLIAM U. MOULTON

Page 215

went to pouting, — this latter so persistently indulged in that my previously benignant features now look as though they were being cast back on my very teeth, so to speak, by a tawdry, wavery, crinkly looking-glass in the last gasp of a boarding-house. But since your voice of yesterday, the eyes of me are lit again, and the whole face beams like radiant summer time. No wonder you continue in indifferent health. It's a judgment on you for your neglect of me. Now you'll begin to improve. And you can get into perfect health by strictly maintaining this rigorous course of writing to me. Heroic treatment, of a truth! . . ."

One of the entries in the diary of the winter reads:

"Could hardly get to the Browning Society, where I read 'A Toccata of Galuppi's.' Mr. Moulton seemed interested about the reading, and I read him the 'Toccata' after dinner, and other poems. A beautiful evening."

Strangely enough this was Mr. Moulton's last evening of being in health. The next day he was taken ill, and on February 19, 1898, he passed into "the life more abundant." The funeral service was read by the Rev. E. Winchester Donald, rector of Trinity, and Mrs.

Moulton more than once spoke of the kindness and sympathy which he showed to her at this time. She wrote in her diary: "Dr. Donald called; he is, it seems to me, a nobly good man." Her daughter was with her, and her many friends were about her. Numerous were the letters of condolence, and they were full of the genuine feeling which could be called out only by one who was herself so ready and quick to respond to the sorrows of others.

In the summer following Mr. Moulton's death Mrs. Moulton remained in America. Her life was saddened and cumbered with the cares needful in business matters, and on the last day of the year she wrote in her diary: "This sad year which is now ending — how strange a year it has been for me. Mr. Moulton died in February and changed all. I have done nothing, enjoyed nothing. With 1899 I must turn over a new leaf, or give up life and all its uses, altogether." In this mood it was natural that her predisposition to brood upon the problem of death should reassert itself. She writes to William Winter: "No, — my dread of death does not seem to me to be physical, for it is not the pain of death that I ever think of. I hate the idea of extinction, but I could reconcile myself to that; . . . but what I dread most is the to-morrow of death,

— the loneliness of the unclothed soul." And again: "For myself, I have an unutterable and haunting horror of going out into the dark. . . . I always wish I might die at the same moment with some well beloved friend, so that hand and hand we might go into the mystery."

Her literary work, however, continues. She said from time to time that she could not write, and that she should never write a line again; but the poetic instinct was strong, and asserted itself in its own time and way. In a letter to a friend she remarks in passing: "The *Century* has just come with my poem, 'A Rose Pressed in a Book,' and it seems to me to read pretty well." The lyric to which she modestly alludes as reading "pretty well" is beautifully characteristic of some of her choicest poetic qualities: easy and seemingly unconscious mastery of form, delicacy of touch, charming melody, and sincerity of emotion.

Always her correspondence goes on.

T. B. Aldrich to Mrs. Moulton

"Some day I must get you to tell me about Andrew Lang. One night last winter as I sat reading one of his books a kind of ghost, distinct, elusive, rose before me. Out of this impression grew my 'Broken Music.'"

In allusion to his much discussed "Modern Love," George Meredith writes:

George Meredith to Mrs. Moulton

"You are like the northern tribes of the Arabs, in that what you love you love wholly and without ceasing. This poem has been more roundly abused than any other of my much-castigated troop. You help me to think that they are not born offenders, antipathetic to the human mind. Americans who first gave me a reputation for the writing of novels will perhaps ultimately take part in the admission that I can write verse. They may thus carry a reluctant consent in England, when I no longer send out my rhyming note for revision. I have been taught, at least, to set no store upon English opinion in such matters. I would thank you, but gratitude is out of place. There is a feeling hard to verbalize."

Mrs. Moulton to Lloyd Mifflin

"It is five days since I received your 'Slopes of Helicon,' enriched by your kind inscription. I have been too ill to write; but I will no longer postpone the pleasure of telling you how delighted I am to have your charming book. I have already read enough to know that the book will be an abiding pleasure. You are as delightful a lyrist as you are a sonneteer, and I could not give you higher praise. Both the sonnets and lyrics in this volume charm me."

". . . This morning, looking over a shelf of books that have accumulated during my absence, — as books are never forwarded to me, — I find your ' Fields of Dawn,' and also 'Lyrics,' by J. H. Mifflin, for both of which I want to thank you at once. I have a real pleasure to look forward to, for I love your sonnets. Am I right in supposing 'J. H. M.' to be your father, and that you are a poet by inheritance? . . ."

"I am sending a hurried note to tell you how entirely I agree with you about the demand for "cheerful poetry."

"It is worth writing a book to have written the line,

"Made eminent by death,

in that noble poem, 'Peace to the Brave.' The poem entitled 'Herbert Spencer' makes me wonder whether you feel that assurance of the future which he certainly did not feel. . . ."

Lloyd Mifflin to Mrs. Moulton

". . . It is very uplifting, as you say in New England, to have such a genuine letter as yours. You read a book as I do, through at once. No one has said that my mind inclines to visions like Blake's, but I see visions. I used to sit and hold the pen and feel it hovering about, becoming nearer and nearer, till suddenly it came, the complete sonnet. I merely recorded it then. This was always wonderful to me. Where do they come from? Not death itself, to say nothing of our earth, can keep a born poet from writing. I can write a better poem about sunset by not seeing it. . . ."

James Whitcomb Riley to Mrs. Moulton

". . . Very slightly changing R. L. S.'s line,

"This be the verse which ye grave for me,
Home he is where he longed to be;

and very thankful I am to be at home again. True, the mother is away, the old father, too, and a sister, and a brother; but they all seem to be here still, with the happy rest of us,— for we all believe, thank God. And you must take this for answer to your very last question, for I do feel that I know. I know likewise why

fuller assurance has been withheld from us,
lest knowing that, not one of all God's children but would be hurrying to Him ere His
own good time. . . . Always your books are
near at hand. May I tell you that I think
the sonnet is your true voice? Yours is the
deep, strong utterance which belongs, with
the soul-cry in it, as individual to yourself
as Mrs. Browning's to herself. Somewhere
we are to talk poetry together sometime!
. . . Of my book, 'A Child's World,' I
venture to send you Mr. Howells' printed
blessing, . . . so delightfully characteristic (I
think) of his very happiest way of saying things.
And, oh! but I am gloating over a supernal
letter from the Archangel Aldrich! Truly with
hurtling praise and God-speed the heavenly
battlements have loosened on me. . . ."

From the same

"Has it been, and is it being, a beautiful
Christmas season to you? for I have been so
praying, though vexing you with no line of
it in ink. And I've seen two new poems of
yours, and they testify to your loyal love of
this world of ours; so I know at least you
can't be happier till you get to Heaven with
no good word or gift forgotten, and such
profusion! Since my return home I've been

mostly working on pyramids of matter accumulated since my taking to the road. But last night I was struck with a real thought, while I was off guard, so to speak. So I've gone to work on that, and I'll send you the result, if I ever overtake it. . . . Lor! but don't praise unexpected hit the very crazybone of vanity!"

From the same

"How beautiful your new poems are! Oh, yes! Even to vaguely question your Divine Inspirer's ultimate intent! . . . Sometimes I even smilingly think that he Has given you that haunting doubt here that your delight may be all the more ineffable a glory when you find His throne more real a fact than this first world of ours."

Among the pleasant friendships which came into a life whose entire texture seemed woven of friendship and song, was that with Coulson Kernahan, who, though one of the younger men of letters in England, had already made a recognized place. His warmly responsive nature made the two especially sympathetic, and they were alike in their devotion to literature. After the vanishing of the "Marston group," Mrs. Moulton's most intimate London circle came to comprise Sir Bruce and

Lady Seton, with whom she stayed frequently at Durham House, Mr. Kernahan, Mrs. Campbell-Praed, and Herbert E. Clarke. Mr. Kernahan's acquaintance with Mrs. Moulton began from a critique on "Swallow Flights" which he had written for the *Fortnightly*. In it he had said:

"No one who looks upon life with earnest eyes can fail to be touched by the passionate human cry which rings from Mrs. Moulton's poems. No one whose ear is attuned to catch the wail that is to be heard in the maddest, merriest music of the violin, to whom the sound of wind and sea at midnight is like that of innumerable lamentations; no one who, in the movement of a multitude of human beings — be they marching to the bounding music of fife and drum, or hurrying to witness a meeting of the starving unemployed — no one who in all these hears something of 'the still, sad music of humanity,' can read her verses unstirred."

Mr. Kernahan had also emphasized — Mrs. Moulton herself thought somewhat unduly — the strain of sadness in her poems; and had he known her personally at the time he wrote, he would surely not have called her "world-weary and melancholy." The point was one often made by critics, and has been alluded to in an earlier chapter. Partly the melancholy note was due to environment, but more to temperament. Mrs. Moulton almost at the beginning had edited a "gift-book" and the fact is significant of the literary fashions of her youth. The "annuals" and "gift-books" of the second quarter of the nineteenth century were redolent of a sort of pressed-rose sadness, a sort of faded-out reminiscence of belated Byronism; a richly passionate gloom of spirit was held to be necessary to lyric inspiration. By this convention Mrs. Moulton was undoubtedly affected, although by no means to such an extent as was Edgar Allan Poe. With her the cause of the minor cadence was chiefly a temperament which gave a sad quality to her singing as nature has put a plaintive timbre into the notes of certain birds. In writing to Mr. Kernahan about his article, she said: "I always hear the minor chords in nature's music; after the summer, the autumn; after youth, age; after life, death. I happened yesterday to close a poem:

> " O June, dear month of sunshine and of flowers,
>   The affluent year will hold you not again;
>   Once, only once, can youth and love be ours,
>   And after that the autumn and the rain.

Is it not true?" Yet she assured him that she was "often gay."

The numerous letters of Mrs. Moulton to Mr. Kernahan were intimate and full of details of business in regard to publication, with personal matters relating to friends and the like, but through them all runs a thread of comment on literature and life.

"I am simply enchanted with the new book William Morris has printed for Wilfrid Blunt, 'The Love Lyrics and Songs of Proteus.'"

"Yes, I did like that one line in Christina Rossetti's poem:

"... half carol and half cry;

but the rest of it is not good enough for her."

"I have had many violets sent me this year, but far the most fragrant were a bunch left for me to-day with a card on which was written:

" Since one too strange to risk intrusion
Would dare rebuke, nor meet confusion,
Yet fain would — failing long to meet you —
With gentle words and memories greet you,
Sweet Mistress of the Triolet,
Admit, I pray, a violet."

"I am reading, or rather rereading Rossetti's sonnet sequence, 'The House of Life.' How unequal are the sonnets,— some of them so beautiful they fairly thrill one's soul with their charm, but others seem whimsical and far fetched. On the other hand, how glorious, how like a full chord of music is, for instance, 'The Heart's Compass,' and the sestet of 'Last Fire,' and that magnificent sonnet, 'The Dark Glass.'"

"I had a letter this morning from a far-off stranger who tells me that her heart keeps time to my poems. . . . I am expecting my beloved Mrs. Spofford to-day. . . . No sweeter soul than she lives on this earth."

"Recently I sent a rhyme called 'A Whisper to the Moon,' to *The Independent*, and in accepting it Bliss Carman writes: 'I like it, and that line

"'She is thy kindred, and fickle art thou,

is immense. Lines with the lyric quality of that are imperishable. Quite apart from its meaning — its cold meaning — it is poetry. It floods the heart. It carries all before it. There is no stopping it. It is like the opening of the gates of the sea. You often write such lines.' The line does not seem to me at all worth such praise, but all the same the praise pleased me. How lovely it is to have

Louise Chandler Moulton

Page 227

people single out some special phrase to care for!"

"Louise Guiney and I are looking over my poems together. Oh, I wish there were more variety in them. They are good (I hope and think) in form, but they are, almost all, the cry of my heart for the love that I long for, or its protest against the death that I fear. Ah, well, I can only be myself."

In this year appeared Mrs. Moulton's third volume of poems, "At the Wind's Will," the title being taken from Rossetti's "Woodspurge":

> I had walked on at the wind's will, —
> I sat now, for the wind was still.

Of it Mrs. Spofford said:

"Mrs. Moulton's last volume of poems, 'At the Wind's Will,' fitly crowns the literary achievement of the century. It is poetry at high-water mark. Her work exhibited in previous volumes has given her a rank among the foremost poets of the world, and much of the work in 'At the Wind's Will' exceeds in grasp and in surrender, in strength and in beauty, anything she has hitherto published."

So the year wore to a close. Her last record for December in her diary reads: "Now this year of 1899 goes out, — a year in which I have accomplished nothing,— gone back, I fear, in every way. God grant 1900 may be better." In part this was the expression of the melancholy natural to ill health, but it was a characteristic cry from one always too likely to underrate herself. Surely the prayer was granted, for the year 1900 gave her again a spring in Rome and Florence, and was filled with rich and significant experiences.

CHAPTER VIII

1900–1906

. . . One in whom
The spring-tide of her childish years
   Hath never lost its sweet perfume,
   Though knowing well that life hath room
For many blights and many tears. — LOWELL.

In my dreams you are beside me, —
   Still I hear your tender tone;
And your dear eyes light my darkness
   Till I am no more alone:
For with memories I am haunted,
   And the silence seems to beat
With the music of your talking,
   And the coming of your feet. — L. C. M.

THE diary during the early months of the year which opened the new century records as often before many kindnesses in the form of reading for various objects:

"Went in evening to read for the Rev. Mr. Shields, of South Boston."

"In the evening read for the College Club. Mrs. Howe presided. The other readers were Dr. Hale, Dr. Ames, Colonel Higginson,

J. T. Trowbridge, Judge Grant, and Nathan Haskell Dole."

"Read for the Young Men's Christian Association. I read 'In Arcady,' 'The Name on a Door,' and 'A June Song,' of my own verses; then my paper on the Marstons, entitled 'Five Friends.' People seemed pleased."

Among her numerous generous acts were to be reckoned the many times when, without regard to herself, she assisted at readings or gave a reading entirely by herself.

On February 19, the entry is:

"Two years ago this day Mr. Moulton passed out of life. It was my first thought this morning, and the sadness of it has been with me all day."

Mr. Moulton had always been to her a tower of strength. Few men were more highly esteemed by those who knew him, or were more deserving of esteem. He was a man of flawless integrity and the highest sense of honor; a man of vigorous intellect, of clear and definite intellectual grasp, and of a generous and kindly nature. He was not himself fond of society, but he was proud of his wife's success, and ministered to her tastes for travel and social life. His sympathy with the literary life was genuine and strong, and his service to clean and wholesome journalism in his editorial work gave him a lasting claim upon public gratitude, had he chosen to assert it. Upon his sterling worth and fine character Mrs. Moulton had always been able to depend, and life without the consciousness of his presence in the home was a thing different and sadder.

In a letter written about this time Mrs. Moulton again touches upon the old question of social struggle:

"I agree with you as to the inanity of struggle for social prominence. How fine is the passage you quote from Emerson: 'My friends come to me unsought. The great God Himself gave them to me.' That is the way I feel. Any social struggle seems to me so little worth while. It is worth while to know the people who really interest one, — but the others! It is always climbing ladders, and there are always other ladders to climb, and one never gets to the top. And then, what will it be if there is an 'after death'? I wonder? Will there be social ambitions,— the desire to get ahead there? It almost seems as if there must be, if there is the continuity of individual existences, for what could change people's desires and tendencies all at once?"

From various letters to the friend to whom this is written, to whom she wrote often, may be put together here a few extracts. The letters were seldom dated, and it is hardly possible to tell exactly when each was written, but the exact sequence is not of importance.

"And what do you think (*entre nous*) I have been asked to do? To go to Cambridge, England, with a party of friends who have included Mme. Blavatsky, and they are to have some brilliant receptions given them there by the occult folk, or those interested. But I declined."

"Mr. —— goes about asking every one if he has read 'The Story of My Heart,' by Jeffries, which is his latest enthusiasm. After being asked till I was ashamed of saying no, I got the book and read it, finding it the most haunting outcry of pessimism imaginable. When one has read it one feels in the midst of a Godless, hopeless world, where nature is hostile, and the animal kingdom alien, and man alone with his destiny,— a destiny that menaces and appalls him. It is a too powerful book. Jeffries makes one feel, for the moment, that all the happy people are happy only because insensate, and are madly dancing on volcanoes."

"Austin Dobson says: 'I have always admired your sonnets,— a thing I can never manage; but how you do take all Gallometry to be your province!! What are we, poor slaves to canzonets and serenades, to do next?' Very pleasant of him."

"Last Saturday the Boyle O'Reilly monument was unveiled, and I was chosen to crown it with a laurel wreath. It was a wonderful occasion; and President Capen, of Tufts College, gave the most eloquent eulogy to which I ever listened."

"My life is not the beautiful life you think, but it is my soul's steadfast purpose to make it all that you believe it already is. Nothing is of any real consequence save to live up to your very highest ideal. In criticism I made up my mind, long ago, that one should be like Swedenborg's angels, who sought to find the good in everything. Of course, really poor things must be condemned — or what *I* think is better — boycotted; but I do not like what is harsh, prejudiced, one-sided. I would see my possible soul's brother in every man — which all means that I am an optimist."

"Can you tell me what Henry James means by his story, 'The Private Life'? Is it an allegory or what? I never saw anything so impossible to understand."

"You speak of the 'close and near friendships' you have made in your few weeks in Florence,— 'friendships for a lifetime.' That is delightful, only I can't make friendships with new people easily; so if I went I should not have that pleasure."

". . . Before I rose this morning, a special messenger came from the Secretary of the Women Writers' Club (which is giving a magnificent dinner to-night at which Mrs. Humphry Ward presides). Miss Blackburne, the 'Hon. Secretary,' had only heard of my being in London this morning, so she at once sent a messenger to invite me. She entreated me to come; said she wanted me to sit at the head of one of the tables, and preside over that table, etc., etc. She sent a most distinguished list of guests, and oh, I *did* want to go — but I felt so ill I dared not try to go, and I sent an immediate refusal. Many of the authors whom I would like to meet will be among the guests. . . ."

"Here is the little screed . . . about Mrs. Browning. The description was given me

by an English lady who saw Mrs. Browning
very often during Mrs. B.'s last visit to Rome.
To her such rumors as (falsely, I am persuaded) have connected Mr. Browning's name
with that of another marriage would have
seemed an impossible impertinence. Indeed,
when one knows — as I happen to know —
that Mr. Browning was asked to furnish some
letters and some data about Mrs. Browning's
life for Miss Zimmern (who had been requested
to write about her for the Famous Women
Series of Biographies) and refused because he
could not bring himself to speak in detail
of the past which had been so dear, or to share
the sacred letters of his wife with the public,
it hardly seems that he can be contemplating
the offer of the place she, his 'moon of
poets,' held in his life, to another.''

In the "little screed" alluded to was this
description of Mrs. Browning, given in the
words of the friend:

"No, she was *not* what people call beautiful; but she was more and better. I can see
her now, as she lay there on her sofa. I
never saw her sitting up. She was always
in white. She wore white dresses, trimmed
with white lace, with white, fleecy shawls
wrapped round her, and her dark brown hair

used to be let down and fall all about her like
a veil. Her face used to seem to me something already not of the earth — it was so
pale, so pure, and with great dark eyes that
gleamed like stars. Then her voice was so
sweet you never wanted her to stop speaking,
but it was also so low you could only hear it
by listening carefully."

"'Was Mr. Browning there?'

" Oh, yes, and he used to watch her as one
watches who has the most precious object
in the whole world to keep guard over. He
looked out for her comfort as tenderly as a
woman.

" I think there never was another marriage
like that; a marriage that made two poet
souls one forever. Don't you notice how
Browning always speaks of finding again the
'soul of his soul'? It was easy enough to
see that that was just what she was. And
the boy was there, too, a little fellow, with
long golden hair, and I remember how quietly
he used to play, how careful he was not to
disturb his mother. Sometimes he used to
stand for a long time beside her, with her
'spirit-small hand,' as her husband called
it, just playing with his curls. I wonder if
he can have known that she was going away
from him so soon."

From various letters of this time of and to Mrs. Moulton may be taken such bits as these:

Mrs. Moulton to Elihu Vedder

"It was such a pleasure to me in my present loneliness to have a good talk with you last night, and I have been thinking of what you said. You would like a big fortune that you might have leisure to fulfil your dreams, but what if you had the fortune and not the dreams? I would a million times rather be you than any capitalist alive. It seems to me that to do work as the few great men in the world have, that must live, is the supreme joy. When you are dust the world will adore the wonder and majesty and beauty of your pictures. It seems to me that I would starve willingly in an attic, like Chatterton, to leave to the wide future one such legacy."

Walter Pater to Mrs. Moulton

"I read very little contemporary poetry, finding a good deal of it a little falsetto. I found, however, in your elegant and musical volume a sincerity, a simplicity, which stand you as constituting a *cachet*, a distinct note."

Mrs. Moulton to Lady Lindsay

"I am reading, with very unusual interest, 'Blake of Oriel,' by Adeline Sargent. It is a story of fate and of heredity, which sets one thinking and questioning. . . . Is fate also to be complicated by the curse of evil inheritance? Oh, is it fair to give life to one with such an inheritance of evil, and then condemn the sinner for what he does? Is it? . . . Is it a loving God who creates men foreknowing that they will commit spiritual suicide? . . . Are people sinners who are doomed by heredity to sin?"

Arthur Christopher Benson to Mrs. Moulton

"Thank you for what you say of my 'Arthur Hamilton.' It is deeply gratifying to me that the book has ever so slightly interested you. As for the difficulties of the hero, I suppose they are the eternal difficulties. It was like my impudent youth to think that to no one else had the same problem been so unjustly presented before, and to rush wildly into a tourney."

The summer of 1900 Mrs. Moulton passed abroad, going before her London visit for the spring in Italy. She revisited familar haunts in Rome and Florence, and again

was steeped in the enchantment of Italy.
In Rome she loved especially the gardens of
the Villa Ludovisi; and indeed, something in
the solemn spell she felt in the Eternal City
appealed especially to her nature. The roses
and the ruins, the antique and the modern;
churches and altars and temples, and modern
studios and society,— each, in turn, attracted
her. She passed hours in the Vatican galleries;
she was fond of driving on the Pincian in the
late afternoon; she took a child's joy in the
festas; she found delight in the works growing under the hand of artists. Of a visit to
the studio of Mr. Story she related: "I was
looking at a noble statue of Saul, and this,
recalling to me the 'Saul' of Browning, led
me to speak of the dead poet. Mr. Story
then told me of his own last meeting with
Browning, which was at Asolo. It was but
a short time before Browning's death, and the
two old friends were talking over all sorts
of intimate things, and finally Mr. Story
entered his carriage to drive away. Browning, who had bade him good-bye and turned
away, suddenly came back, and reached his
hand into the carriage, grasping that of Story,
and looking into the sculptor's eyes exclaimed,
'Friends for forty years! Forty years without
a break.' Then with a last good-bye he

turned away, and the two friends never met again."

After the London visit, Mrs. Moulton went for the cure at Aix-les-Bains, perhaps as much for the delightful excursions of the neighborhood as in any hope of help for her almost constant ill-health. Thence she went in September to Paris, still in the full glory of its Exposition year. While in Paris she received from Professor Meiklejohn the comments upon her latest volume, "At the Wind's Will." He had fallen into the custom of going over her poems carefully, and of sending her his notes of admiration. "I still maintain," he wrote her on this occasion, "that your brothers are the Elizabethan lyrists, Shakespeare, Fletcher, Vaughan." Some of the comments were these:

"In 'When Love is Young,' the line

" Time has his will of every man,

is in the strong style of the sixteenth century.

"I think the 'Dead Men's Holiday' martial and glorious.

" And the keen air stung all their lips like wine,

is the kind of line when Nature has taken the pen into her own hand.

"What an exquisite stanza is this in 'The Summer's Queen':

> " You sow the fields with lilies — wake the choir
> Of summer birds to chorus of delight;
> Yours is the year's deep rapture — yours the fire
> That burns the West, and ushers in the night.

"The line

> " Yet done with striving, and foreclosed of care,

in the sonnet entitled 'At Rest' is as good as anything of Drayton's. You know his sonnet,

> " Since there 's no help, come, let us kiss and part!

> " Mocked by a day that shines no more on thee,

in the sonnet called 'The New Year Dawns,' is the very truth in the strong simplicity of the Elizabethan age.

"What a wonderful line is the last one of the sonnet, 'The Song of the Stars':

> " The waking rapture, and the fair, far place."

The serenity and sweetness of Longfellow's verse are the natural expression of a life sweet and serene; and in the work of Mrs. Moulton the beauty of her work was in no less a measure the inevitable outcome of her character. She wrote so spontaneously that her poems seemed, as she used to say, "to come to her," and although she never spared the most careful polishing, yet her song seemed to spring without effort and almost without conscious prevision.

The literary life was to her in its outward aspect chiefly a matter of fit and harmonious companionship. She declared that she thought "the great charm of a literary life was that it made one acquainted with so many delightful people." Her warm sense of the personality and characteristics of the writers whom she met in London has been alluded to already, and some of her words about them have been quoted in a former chapter. Those who enjoyed the privilege of chatting with her in her morning-room were never tired of hearing her give her impressions of distinguished authors.

"George Meredith's talk," she said on one occasion, "is like his books, it is so scintillating, so epigrammatic. In talking with him you have to be swiftly attentive or you will miss some allusion or witticism, and seem disreputably inattentive."

"Thomas Hardy," she said again, "has the face, I think, which one would expect from his books. His forehead is so large and so fine that it seems to be half his face. His blue eyes are kindly, but they are extremely shrewd. You feel that he sees everything, and that because he would always understand he would always forgive. I have heard him called the shyest man in London, but he never impressed me so."

"I did not find George Eliot so plain a person as she is ordinarily represented," she replied to a question about that author. "To me she seemed to have a singularly interesting face and a lovely smile; and one distinctive trait, one peculiarly her own, was a very gentle and sweet deference of manner. In any difference of opinion, she always began by agreeing with the person with whom she was conversing, as 'I quite see that, but don't you think —' and then there would follow a statement so supremely convincing, so comprehensive, so true, so sweetly suggestive, that one could not help being convinced. It was like a fair mist over a background of the greatest strength."

Christmas was always a season of much activity at No. 28 Rutland Square. The tokens which Mrs. Moulton sent to friends kept her and Katy busy long in arranging and sending; and in turn came gifts from far and near. With her generous and friendly spirit she was fully in sympathy with the spirit of the time. Among her Christmas gifts on this year, was one from Louise Imogen Guiney, with these charming and delicately humorous verses:

TO LOUISE CHANDLER MOULTON

WITH A THERMOMETER AT CHRISTMAS.

Behold, good Hermes! (once a god
With errand-winglets crowned and shod),
Your silvern, sensitive, slim rod,
   Still potent, still surviving;
Chill mimic of the chilly sky,
Crouched, chin on knee, morose and sly,
Where, in my luthern window's eye,
   The Christmas snows are driving.
But if beside her heart you were,
And over you the smile of her,
Oh, never might the north-wind stir,
   Or gleaming frost benumb her!
For you, of old, love warmth and light,
And in the calendar's despite,
This moment leaping to your height,
   I know you'd swear 't is summer!

On January 1, 1901, Mrs. Moulton records in her diary:

"Wrote a sonnet, the first in nearly or quite two years, beginning, 'Once more the New Year mocks me with its scorn.'"

When the poem was published, "New Year" had been changed to "morning."

The summer of this year found her again in London. Her health was seriously affected, and at times she was a great sufferer; but when she was able to go about among her friends she was as full of spirit as ever. Indeed, the diary gives a surprising list of festivities which she attended.

"Went to Lady Wynford's charming luncheon."

"Went to Edward Clifford's to see pictures, and had the loveliest evening."

"Went to Archdeacon Wilberforce's, Mrs. Meynell's, and Mrs. Clifford's, and dined at Annie Lane's."

"Lunch at Sir Richard Burton's at Hampstead Heath. Lady Burton, who can never sit up, because of spinal trouble, was charming."

"Some one — a lady who left no name — brought me charming roses. A good many guests — Lady Wynford, Mrs. Sutherland Orr, Canon Bell, and George Moore among them."

"Went to Lord Iddesleigh's. He gave me his first book, 'Belinda Fitzwarren.'"

To this summer belongs the following letter, which is interesting not only in itself, but also as illustrating how the old questions of religion followed Mrs. Moulton through life:

Dr. E. Winchester Donald to Mrs. Moulton

"JULY 9, 1901.

" . . . This place is a paradise. The Thames, from Windsor to Henley, is a beautiful dream, sailing up and down — no churches, no responsibilities. Consequently we New Englanders need not urge that it is dangerous to linger long upon its bosom. If there be no physical miasma rising from these waters, I fear there is an ethical one. . . . You are very kind and very generous. Your gift is very acceptable to us, and in my own name and that of those whom the Church is trying to help, I thank you with all my heart. What you have told me of the perplexities that beset you is more than simply interesting,— it is also revelatory of what, I fancy, is not uncommon among the thoughtful folk. But why not fall back deliberately on worship as distinguished from satisfactory precision of opinion or belief? I should not be surprised to learn that prayer has tided many people over the bar of intellectual perplexity into the harbor of a reasonable faith. Indeed, I know it has. The instinct of humanity is to worship and fall down before the Lord, our Maker. Why should we insist on having a precisely formulated proposition as respects the nature of that Lord before we worship? Prayer and praise form the sole common meeting-ground of humanity. Why not come back to the Church, not as a thoroughly satisfied holder of accurately stated formulas, but as a soul eager to gain whatever of help, hope, or comfort the Church has to give? You would never repent this, I am confident. My strong wish, never stronger than to-day, is that all of us may be receiving from God what God is only ready to give. For our reasoned opinions we must be intellectually intrepid and industrious. For our possession of the peace that passeth understanding we must be spiritually receptive and responsive."

After Mrs. Moulton's return to Boston in the autumn, the diary shows the old round of engagements, of visits from friends, of interest in the new books, and the writing and receiving of innumerable letters. Mrs. Alice Meynell came to Boston in the winter as the guest of Mrs. James T. Fields, and to her Mrs. Moulton gave a luncheon. The Emerson-Browning club gave a pleasant reception in Mrs. Moulton's honor, at which by request she read "The Secret of Arcady"; at one of Mrs. Mosher's "Travel-talks" she read by invitation "The Roses of La Garraye"; and with occasions of this sort the winter was dotted.

In a note written that spring to Mrs. John Lane is this pleasant passage:

"Frances Willard's mother was in her eighties, — she was on her death-bed — it was, I think, the day before she died, and her daughter said to her, 'Well, mother, if you had your life to live over again, I don't think you would want to do anything differently from what you have done.' The dear old lady turned her gray head on the pillow, and smiled, and said, 'Oh, yes; if I had my life to live over again, I would praise a great deal more and blame a great deal less.' I always thought it lovely to have felt and said."

In London in this summer of 1902 she notes in her diary that she went to the dinner of the Women Writers. Later, she was given a luncheon by the Society of American Women in London. She sat, of course, on the right of the president, Mrs. Griffin, and next to her was placed Lady Annesley, "who seemed to me," she said afterward, "the most beautiful woman I had ever seen." She gave a little dinner to which she invited Whistler, who accepted in the following terms:

J. McNeill Whistler to Mrs. Moulton

96 CHEYNE ROAD.

DEAR LOUISE: I accept your invitation
with great pleasure, and how kind and con-
siderate of you to make it eight-thirty. I
really believe I shall reach you, not only in
good time, but in the unruffled state of mind
and body that is utterly done away with in
the usual scramble across country, racing
hopelessly for the "quarter to." . . .

Yours sincerely,

J. McN. W.

When in her Boston home Mrs. Moulton
was seldom, in later years, allured far afield.
She thought little of a journey to Europe, but
avoided even an hour's journey "out of town."
She had in London, however, come to be fond
of the lady who became Mrs. Truman J.
Martin, of Buffalo, N. Y., and to her had
written the lyric, "A Song for Rosalys";
and she made an exception to her usual custom to visit her friend in her American home.
A Buffalo journal remarks on the occurrence
with the true floridness of society journalism:

"The event of the week *par excellence* has
been the arrival in Buffalo of that gifted writer
and eminent woman — Mrs. Louise Chandler

Moulton of Boston. Mrs. Moulton arrived
on Monday evening, and is the guest of her
friend, Mrs. Truman J. Martin of North
Street, where she is resting after a season
of excessive literary work and many social
obligations. . . . Mrs. Moulton has a striking
personality. The years have touched lightly
her heart and features, her strongest characteristic being a heartiness and sincerity and
warmth that come to a great soul who has
enjoyed and suffered much and who has
dipped into the deepest of life's grand experiences. She dresses handsomely and somewhat
picturesquely, elegant laces and rich velvet
and silks forming themselves into her expres-
sive attire."

The reporter goes on to describe a reception
given to Mrs. Moulton by her hostess at
which a local club known as the Scribblers
was represented:

"Flowers were everywhere in the house,
bowls and vases of white carnations. 'The
Scribblers" flowers, and roses and lilies for
'Rosalys,' Mrs. Martin's middle name, and
which she still retains — 'Charlotte Rosalys
Jones,' as her pen name. . . . Mrs. Moulton
was dressed in black satin, with elegant rose-
point lace and diamonds. . . . The real de-

light of the afternoon came when Mrs. Moulton took up a little bundle of her poems, special selections of Mrs. Martin's, and read with great expression some of the sublime, pathetic, and passionate thoughts that have endeared this writer to the English reading world and placed her among the foremost of American writers. Mrs. Moulton's voice is of peculiar timbre, and reveals to the intelligent listener a character of the finest mould, suffering intensely through the inevitable decrees of a fate not too kind to the most favored, and a wealth of love and devotion that is immeasurable."

The hostess might be English, but the description of the entertainment could hardly be more American.

Mrs. Moulton mentioned that during this visit she met Mrs. Charles Rohlfs (Anna Katherine Green), and had an opportunity of saying that she had enjoyed that writer's novels. Like Mrs. Browning, who declared that she "slept with her pillows stuffed with novels," Mrs. Moulton was a confirmed reader of fiction. She read them at seventy with the zest of seventeen, and took "cruel endings" quite to heart.

Among the letters of the winter is an amusing note from Secretary John Hay, accompanying a copy of the "Battle of the Books," and saying: "Don't ask how I obtained it! I am proud to say in a strictly dishonest manner!" An invitation from Miss Anne Whitney, too, asking her to dine, and assuring her that she "will meet some friends without strikingly bad traits"; and many epistles from which pleasant bits might be taken. An interesting letter from Alice Brown refers to the subject of death, and in allusion to her friend, Louise Imogen Guiney, Miss Brown says: "So if you go before Louise and me, it will only be to begin another spring somewhere else, — gay as the daffodils. I hope you 'll keep your habit of singing there, and we shall all love to love and love to serve." A letter of Bliss Carman's thus refers to Miss Guiney:

Bliss Carman to Mrs. Moulton

". . . Have you seen that perfect thing of Louise Imogen Guiney's with the lines, —

"And children without laughter lead
The war-horse to the watering.

"Is n't that the gold of poetry? She ought to have a triumph on the Common, and a window in Memorial Hall. . . . Do you see that faun of Auburndale?"

On New Year's Day, 1903, the diary records: "First of all I wrote a sonnet — 'Why Do I never See You in My Dreams?'"

The summer was passed in London as usual, but with, if possible, more festivities than ever. The diary records:

"Went to Lady Seton's luncheon party — of I think twenty — a very pleasant affair in honor of Mr. Howells and his daughter. I sat next to Mr. Howells and had a good talk with him."

"Went to the luncheon at the Cecil, given by the Society of American Women in London in honor of Ambassador and Mrs. Reid and Mr. and Mrs. Longworth."

"Went in the evening to the Women Writers' dinner. I sat at Mrs. Craigie's table."

"Went to the Lyceum Club Saturday dinner. Lady Frances Balfour presided."

"Went to the Baroness Burdett-Coutts' garden-party. Oh, Holly Lodge is such a beautiful place!"

"Went to Irving's dinner at the New Gallery. Sir Edward Russell, editor of the *Daily Post*, Liverpool, took me out; and a delightful companion he was."

"Many guests: Mrs. Wilberforce, Lady Henry Somerset, Mrs. Henniker, the Pearsall Smiths, William Watson, Oswald Crawfurd, 'Michael Field' (that is to say Miss Bradley and Miss Cooper), Violet Hunt, Mr. and Mrs. Clement Shorter, Archdeacon and Mrs. Wilberforce, and many more."

As the years went on, bringing her to the verge of seventy, Mrs. Moulton's literary activity naturally grew greatly less. The record of her life for the following years was largely a record of friendships, with the enjoyments and honors which belonged to her place among American writers. She was asked often to write her reminiscences of the many distinguished people she had known, but always declined. "I have, alas! kept no records," she wrote to one editor. She was naturally asked to be present at any literary function of importance. She was a guest at the dinner given by the New England Women's Club in 1905, in honor of Mrs. Howe's eighty-fifth birthday, and notes that it was "a brilliant meeting," and adding: "Mrs. Howe had written a gay little poem in response, wonderful woman that she is." The dinner given in honor of Mark Twain's seventieth birthday was the last great occasion of the kind which

she attended. In the following year she returned from Europe just too late to join in
the dinner given by the Harpers on the seventieth birthday of Dr. Alden. Not only for her
literary standing and as an old friend of Dr.
Alden would it have been appropriate for her
to be present on this occasion; but she might
also have appeared as his first contributor, as
some thirty years earlier, Dr. Alden's first
official act upon assuming the chair as editor
of *Harper's Magazine* had been to accept a
contribution from Mrs. Moulton.

In the letters of this period are to be found
the truest records of what most interested Mrs.
Moulton and best expressed her personality.
Unfortunately she often asked that her letters
should be destroyed, so that no selection which
may now be brought together does her complete justice. The letters she received, however, reflect in many ways those to which they
replied; and extracts from them may be left
to speak for themselves.

Louise Imogen Guiney to Mrs. Moulton

". . . On an awfully wild and windy day
of last week I struck off for Highgate over
Hampstead Heath, and got so drenched addi-
tionally in the memories of the men who reign
over me, Lamb, Coleridge, Keats, Shelley,

and Hunt, that I declare now I must live there a while. Coleridge's tomb I knew to be under the crypt of the Grammar School, and I found the Gilmans' house where he died, thanks to the only knowledge that I seem to have had from everlasting. The tomb is a queer piece of masonry, so placed that you may put your hand within an inch of his coffin. After some exploring and inquiring, George Eliot's grave turned up in the new grounds of Highgate Cemetery, where I suppose poor Philip Marston's must be. Her grave is an entirely unconventional affair, to the memory of Mary Ann Cross. I caught myself wondering whether there were any special reason for laying that great soul (here is some theological inaccuracy!) in so narrow and crowded a space, when suddenly I shifted my position, and saw that she was lying directly at the feet of George Henry Lewes, born August 4, 1817, died December 30, 1878. It gave me a queer sensation, I tell you, for Lewes' marble is half hidden and not visible from the path. If it were George Eliot's wish, honor to Mr. Cross for carrying it out!"

"Some agreeable witchery, sure to be transient, is about me to-day, for I 've made a 'pome,' the first since winter, and patched up a trivial old one, — both of which I send you as a slight token that I may get out of Bedlam yet. The sonnet I want you to cherish, it is so abominably pessimistic. . . . "

"I have been luxuriating in 'Atalanta.' . . . That is my springtime. There is no such music and motion and solemn gladness anywhere in modern verse. In a year or two more I shall know it by heart from cover to cover. . . . And here is England knee-deep in green and daisies; England piled with ruined Abbey walls."

"I have two refreshments to chronicle, — one is Irving's 'Becket,' and not the stockstill, curiously inefficient play, but just Irving's 'Becket,' otherwise 'St. Thomas of Canterbury,' a flash and a breath from Heaven. Where does that actor get his gift of everything spiritual and supernatural? His charm to me is that he has great moral power, — either inherent from the noble mind . . . or else acquired by art so subtle that I never got hold of the like. . . . Surely, not everybody can see so into a character . . . and measure its astonishing depth in humanity and divinity."

Archdeacon Wilberforce to Mrs. Moulton

"Dear Mrs. Chandler-Moulton: Thank you for your letter. On page 237, of the book

17

I send you, I have answered your question 'Why cannot God make people good in the first instance.' Because even God can only make things by means of the process by which they become what they are. God could not make a hundred-year-old tree in your garden in one minute. He cannot make a moral being except through the processes by means of which a moral being becomes what he is. What does Walt Whitman say?

" Our life is closed, our life begins.

And again:

" In the divine ship, the World hasting Time and Space,
All People of the globe together sail, sail the same voyage, are bound for the same destination. . . ."

Miss Robbins to Mrs. Moulton

96 MT. VERNON ST.,
January 23, 1906.

MY DEAR MRS. MOULTON: This little note from Dean Hodges belongs to you rather than to me. If you had never written anything else all your life but this beautiful "Help Thou Mine Unbelief," you have done something worth living for, something truly great.

And now to explain a little. I was glad to meet Dean Hodges at your house, and I asked him if among your poems he knew this one that I so prized. I told him that I had shown it to Dr. Momerie, who murmured, after reading it: "It is finer, it is, than 'Lead, Kindly Light.'" Dr. Momerie then went on to say there were only half a dozen good hymns, and that this was one of them. As Dean Hodges did not know the poem, I offered to copy it for him, as I have done for several people before, and now this is his reply. Such praise from such a man is praise indeed!

I had such an interesting time at your house, meeting such interesting people, but what I wanted most was a *tête-à-tête* with my interesting hostess. I always want to know you better.

Believe me, dear Mrs. Moulton,

Always yours,

JULIA ROBBINS.

Dean Hodges to Miss Robbins

[*Enclosed*]

THE DEANERY, CAMBRIDGE,
January 22, 1906.

DEAR MISS ROBBINS: I cannot thank you enough for these devout and helpful verses of Mrs. Moulton's. I have read and re-read them, — every time with new appreciation. They belong to the great hymns.

It was a pleasure to meet you, and one I hope to have again.

Faithfully yours,

GEORGE HODGES.

Dr. Hale to Mrs. Moulton

APRIL 5, 1906.

DEAR MRS. MOULTON: I thank you indeed for the kind expression of memories and hopes which calls up so much from the past and looks forward so cheerfully into the future. . . . No, as life goes on with us, we do not rest as often as I should like. But that is the special good of a milestone like this, — it gives us a chance to look backward and forward.

This note has carried me back to an old friend, Phillips, the publisher, who died too early for the rest of us. You will not remember it, but he introduced me to you. I wonder if you can know how highly he prized your literary work?

With thanks for your kind note, dear Mrs. Moulton,

I am always yours,
EDWARD EVERETT HALE.

Mrs. Moulton's visit to London in the summer of 1906 was her last. While her health forced her to decline most invitations, she still saw her numerous friends in quiet, intimate ways, and was made to feel their abiding affection.

On her birthday of this year she received, with a single red rose, this poem from the late Arthur Upson:

Does a rose at the bud-time falter
    To think of the Junes gone by?
Shall our love of the red rose alter
    Because it so soon must die?

Nay, for the beauty lingers
    Though the symbols pass away —
The rose that fades in my fingers,
    The June that will not stay.

I used to mourn their fleetness,
    But years have taught me this:
A memory wakes their sweetness,
    The hope of them, their bliss.

They are not themselves the treasure,
    But they signal and they suggest
Imperishable pleasure,
    Inviolable rest!

Among the Christmas gifts which she made this year was a copy of "At the Wind's Will," which she sent to Miss Sarah Holland Adams, the accomplished essayist and translator from the German.   It was thus acknowledged:

Miss Adams to Mrs. Moulton

"DEAR MRS. MOULTON: Your beautiful little book is a dear thing. I thank you for sympathy in the loss of my only brother. I

that we are, even now, continually with Him in the great Forever, embosomed in the infinite power and purity." In Mrs. Moulton's own words, it is only

From life to Life

that we pass.

In retrospective glance, how beautiful are these closing months of her sojourn on earth! They were filled to the last with love and friendship, and sweet thought. Mrs. Moulton's health was constantly failing from this winter of 1907 until she passed through the "Gleaming Gates" in August of 1908, but so gently imperceptible was the decline that even through this winter she half planned to go to London again in the spring. In a little meditation on the nature of life which T. P. O'Connor induced her to write for his journal about this time, under the caption of "My Faith and My Works," she said:

"There must be always 'the still, sad music of humanity'— the expression of the mind that foresees, of the heart that aches with foreknowledge. One would not ignore the gladness of the dawn, the strong splendor of the mid-day sun; but, all the same, the shadows lengthen, and the day wears late.

"And yet the dawn comes again after the

night; and one has faith — or is it hope rather than faith? — that the new world which swims into the ken of the spirit to whom Death gives wings, may be fairer even than the dear familiar earth — that, somewhere, somehow, we may find again the long-lost; or meet the long-desired, the un-found, who forever evaded our reach in this mocking sphere, where we have never been quite at home, because, after all, we are but travellers, and this is but our hostelry, and not our permanent abode."

"My best reward has been the friendships that my slight work has won for me," she had said; and the assurance of these did not fail her to the end.

In the article just quoted she said of her work:

"I have written many times more prose than verse, but it is my verse which is most absolutely *me*, and for which I would rather that you should care. Some critics assert that the sonnet is an artificial form of expression. Is it? I only know that no other seems to me so intimate — in no other can I so sincerely utter the heart's cry of despair or of longing — the soul's aspiration toward that which is eternal.

"Am I a realist? I think I am; but who was it who said that the sky is not less real than the mud?"

The death of her old friend, Mr. Aldrich, greatly moved her, and in her diary for March 20, 1907, she records:

"Indoors all day; an awful wind storm, and the day was made sad by the news in the morning's paper of T. B. Aldrich's death yesterday, in the late afternoon. Oh, how sad death seems. Aldrich was seventy last November. How soon we, his contemporaries, shall all be gone. His death seems to darken everything."

Two days later she writes:

"Went to the funeral services of T. B. Aldrich, at Arlington Street Church. The services, the music, and Mr. Frothingham's reading, were most impressive and beautiful. . . . In the evening came Mr. Stedman to see me. His visit was a real pleasure, I had not seen him for so long."

This must have been the last meeting between Mrs. Moulton and Mr. Stedman after their almost life-long friendship.

To Mrs. Aldrich she wrote:

Mrs. Moulton to Mrs. Aldrich

28 RUTLAND SQUARE,
March 30, 1907.

DEAR MRS. ALDRICH: I cannot tell you how my talk with you a few days ago brought the long past back to me. How I wish I could put into words a picture of your poet as I saw him first. I was in New York for a visit, and was invited for an afternoon to an out-of-town place, where a poet-friend and his wife were staying. Other interesting people were there, but *the* one I remember was T. B. A. His poems had charmed me, and to me he was not only their author, but their embodiment. Had it been otherwise, I should have felt bereft of an ideal; but he was all I had imagined and more. I saw him alive with the splendor of youth, rich, even then, in achievement, and richer still in hope and dreams,— a combination of knight and poet. He escorted me back to New York, I remember, and the charm of his presence and his conversation still lingers in my memory. Ever since then I have kept in touch with his work and loved it. His personality attracted every one who met him, and his generous kindness and appreciation were a joy to those who sought his sympathy.

I remember the pleasure with which my poet-friend, Frederic Lawrence Knowles, told me of a kind invitation to call on Mr. Aldrich, and the yet more enthusiastic delight with which he afterward described the interview. He found his gracious and graceful host to be so wise, sympathetic, hopeful, and suggestive, all that he had hoped for and more. I think every young poet who had the happiness of meeting him could bear similar testimony.

I saw him last on the twelfth of January, 1907, so short a time before his death, and yet he seemed so alert and alive, so interesting, so entirely what he was when I knew him first that one could not have dreamed that the end was near. The only consolation for a loss that will be so widely felt is in the legacy he has left to the world of immortal charm and beauty,— the work that will not die.

Yours most sincerely,
LOUISE CHANDLER MOULTON.

The last sonnet which Mrs. Moulton wrote was for the birthday of Mrs. Howe.

TO JULIA WARD HOWE

ON HER EIGHTY-SEVENTH BIRTHDAY, MAY 27, 1907

Youth is thy gift — the youth that baffles Time,
  And smiles derisively at vanished years.
  Since the long past the present more endears,

And life but ripens in its golden prime,
Who knows to what proud heights thou still may'st climb —
   What summoning call thy listening spirit hears —
   What triumphs wait, ere conquering death appears —
What magic beauty thou may'st lend to rhyme?

Sovereign of Love and May, we kiss the hand
   Such noble work has wrought, and add our bays
To those with which the world has crowned thy brow:
Thy subjects we, in this the happy land,
   Thy presence gladdens, and thy gracious ways
Enchant — Queen of the Long-Ago and Now.

During the summer Mrs. Moulton was for
the most part in her morning-room, surrounded by her favorite books, her papers,
her letters, attended by the faithful Katy, and
remembered constantly with flowers and tokens
from friends. She cherished until quite mid-
summer the hope of joining the Schaefers,
who were in Europe; but in reply to their
urgent wish to return and be with her, she
begged that they would not cut short their
trip, as it would distress her to feel that they
were in Boston during the hot weather. To
a friend who remained in town and who saw
her every day, she said: "It would make me
really ill to have Florence and Will come into
this hot town. I should only feel how uncomfortable they must be, dear as they are
to wish to come for my sake. With letters
and the cable, we are in touch all the time."

It was, on the whole, a pleasant season, although she was often uncomfortable if not actually in pain. Friends urged her to come into the country, but to this she did not feel equal. Mrs. Spofford had met with an accident, but before the summer was over was able to resume her visits; and more than anything else her companionship brightened the days.

The autumn brought back the accustomed circle, and in October came the following letter from Dr. Ames:

Dr. Ames to Mrs. Moulton

12 CHESTNUT ST., BOSTON,
October 24, 1907.

MY DEAR FRIEND: I am somewhat foot-fast; but very far from indifferent, and you will never know how often your name is called as I tell my rosary beads.

I wonder if you find comfort, as I often do, in the thought that all true and honorable human friendship is representative of its inspiring source, and that we should not thus care for each other, and wish each other's highest welfare, if our hearts were not in receptive touch with a Heart still greater, purer, and more loving? Can you rest in the imperfect good will of your friends and yet distrust its Origin and Fountain?

I appreciate and share your perplexity over the world's "Vast glooms of woe and sin." But, when most weary and heavy-laden with all our common burden of sorrow and shame, I find some measure of strength and peace in the example and spirit of One who knew and felt it all, One who could gather into a heart of boundless compassion all the blind and struggling multitudes, and could yet trust all the more fully to the Father's love for all, because He felt that love in His own.

The problem of evil — my evil, yours, everybody's — was not solved by Him with any reasoning; it was simply met and over-matched by faith which saw all finite things held in the Infinite, as all the stars are held in space.

Did sin abound? Grace did much more abound. To that superabounding grace I commit all our needy souls. I know no other resource. I need no other.

> Not all the sins that we have wrought
> So much His tender mercies grieve
> As that unkind, injurious thought
> That He's not willing to forgive.

As for unanswered questions,— let them rest. They rest while you sleep; let them rest while you wake. In opening a window to look out, we shall let in the blessed light of heaven. How many hearts have found this true! Did any ever find it untrue? To escape from self-attention is the sure cure of morbid, self-consuming thoughts and moods. . . .

While you and I are waiting for the sunset gun, what use can we make of our afternoon except to welcome the sacred horizontal light, which shows us how our resources and energies can best be applied to the welfare of others? If in considering our remaining opportunities and duties, we may partly forget our own private troubles, that will be salvation, will it not? We may be sure that all the happiness we try to secure for others will return to ourselves redoubled. You would say this to another, why not say it insistently to yourself.

Faithfully yours,
CHARLES GORDON AMES.

In November her daughter and son-in-law arrived, and from that time did not leave her. There were happy days in which Mrs. Moulton was able to drive, although these were rare, and as the winter wore on she was less and less able to see friends. The last letter she ever wrote, save for some brief words to Mrs. Spofford, written when she could with difficulty hold a pen, was one to Archdeacon

Wilberforce, and even this was left unfinished.
It was entirely concerned with religious ques-
tionings.

The entries in her diary became few and
irregular. There is a pathetic beauty in the
fact that the latest complete record, in the
early summer of 1908, is a mention of a visit
from "dear Hal," Mrs. Spofford. The very
last was simply the words "Florence and
Will," which fitly closed the record which
had extended over more than a quarter of a
century.

Hardly a month before her death Colonel
Higginson wrote to her that he felt that in
her execution she excelled all other American women-poets. She had questioned him
of death, and he replied: "Your question
touches depths. I never in my life felt any
fear of death, as such. I never think of my
friends as buried."

The transition came on Monday, August 10,
1908. On the Friday before she had seemed
better, and Mrs. Spofford, who was with her
on that day, remarked afterward that "It was
delightful to hear her repeat her lyric, 'Roses.'"

> Roses that briefly live,
> Joy is your dower;
> Blest be the fates that give
> One perfect hour;

> For, though too soon you die,
>   In your dust glows
> Something the passer-by
>   Knows was a rose.

"Velvet-soft in this," Mrs. Spofford continued, "her voice had a ringing gayety whose strange undertone was sorrow when reciting, 'Bend Low, O Dusky Night.'"

On Saturday she seemed still her old self, but on Sunday afternoon she became unconscious, and on the morning following came release. So peaceful was the transition that to the watchers it was as if she only passed from sleep into a deeper peace. The lines of the late Father Tabb might almost seem to have been written to describe that fitting end:

> Death seemed afraid to wake her,
>   For traversing the deep
> When hence he came to take her,
>   He kept her fast asleep.
> And happy in her dreaming
>   Of many a risk to run,
> She woke with rapture beaming,
>   To find the voyage done.

The funeral service was held three days later. Friends had sent masses of flowers, and among them she rested, never more beautiful, with only peace on the still face. An incident slight, but at such a moment touching, marked the removal of the casket from

LOUISE CHANDLER MOULTON'S GRAVE IN MOUNT AUBURN, CAMBRIDGE, MASS.

Page 275

the house. As it was borne down the steps a
superb golden butterfly flew on just before it,
as if it were a visible symbol of the rich spirit
now "loosed upon the air." The committal
was at Mount Auburn, where her grave is
beside that of Mr. Moulton. A beautiful
Celtic cross marks the spot where rests all
that was mortal of one of the sweetest and
most genuine singers of all her century.

The letters of sympathy sent to Mrs. Schaefer were many and spontaneous, full of individual feeling and of a sense of personal loss
on the part of the writers. "I shall always
feel grateful for the privilege of Mrs. Moulton's
friendship," wrote the Rev. Albert B. Shields,
then rector of the Church of the Redeemer.
"One of the kindest friends I ever had,"
wrote Professor Evans, of Tufts College;
"no one that I have known had a greater
capacity than she for making close friends."
"No one loved your mother as I did," was the
word from Coulson Kernahan, "and her passing leaves me lonelier and sadder than I can
say." Mrs. Margaret Deland spoke of her
"nature so generous, so full of the appreciation of beauty, and of such unfailing human
kindness." Mrs. Spofford, so long and so
closely her friend, said simply: "I miss her
more and more as the days go by. I miss

her sympathy, her comradeship. . . . She was inspiringly good and dear to me; and her love will go with me to the last."

Such extracts might be multiplied, but they are not needed. The affection she felt and inspired must live in the hearts of her friends, and such letters are almost too tender and intimate to be put into cold print.

Mrs. John Lane, now of London, but in former years known in Boston as Miss Eichberg, one of the intimates of 28 Rutland Square, has written the following reminiscences of Mrs. Moulton, between whom and herself long existed a warm friendship:

"An anecdote told by Mrs. Moulton about Thomas Carlyle and his wife has been going the rounds of the press since her death, coming thus to my notice. I only partially recognize it as one she had often told me. The true version of it is as follows: Mrs. Moulton had it from her friend, Lady Ashburton, who was also a friend of Carlyle and his wife. It seems that Lady Ashburton had invited the Carlyles to visit her. There was a large house-party of people congenial to the great man, and one day after dinner Lady Ashburton prevailed on Carlyle to read aloud some passages from the 'French Revolution.'

From reading, Carlyle, carried away by his subject, continued a discourse independent of his own work, which was so brilliant and eloquent that his hearers were profoundly impressed. After he had ceased and it was time for all to separate for the night, they went, in turn, to express to him their appreciation. The only person who did not do this was his wife, and as Carlyle stood as if expectant, Lady Ashburton said rather impulsively to Mrs. Carlyle: 'Why don't you speak to him? Your praise means more to him than that of all the rest, and only see how he has moved them!' 'Ah, yes,' replied Mrs. Carlyle, 'but they don't have to live with him.'"

"I first met Mrs. Moulton in London in the early eighties. I had a letter of introduction to her from a common Boston friend. She was then in the beginning of her London success, knowing everybody in the literary world worth knowing, and extending her simple and charming hospitality to very great people indeed. To go to her Fridays was always to meet men and women whose names are famous on two continents. To a young girl as I was, brought up with a deep veneration for all things literary in England, it was a wonderful opportunity to come face to face, through her kindness, with the curious phases of art and literature of that period.

"These movements were the outcome of the pre-Raphaelite, the outward aspects of that erratic and distinguished society, and its artificial simplicity. It was enough to impress any one coming from so conventional a city as Boston. Perhaps the deepest impression made on me was by Philip Bourke Marston, for I remember how Mrs. Moulton brought him to see us, and my father, Julius Eichberg, played for him on the violin. Never shall I forget the picture as he sat there listening, his head supported by his hand, and the various expressions evoked by the music passing over his face.

"It was undoubtedly through Mrs. Moulton that the younger English poets of those earlier days won American recognition. Many of these who have now an assured place in literature were first known in America through her introduction. As I remember now, it was she who first unfolded to me the splendid, stately perfection and the profound thought of William Watson, and I can still hear her lovely voice as she recited to me that wonderful poem of his, 'World-Strangeness.' It was she who first read to me 'The Ballad of a Nun,' by John Davidson, and that moving and tragic poem by Rosamond Marriott, '*Le Mauvais Larron.*'

"I remember going with Mrs. Moulton to Miss Ingelow's. Once I remember, when James Russell Lowell was first accredited Minister to the Court of St. James, and had just arrived in London, we met him at Miss Ingelow's. He was evidently a stranger to the hostess and to all her guests, and I recall his talking to her, holding in his hand a cup of tea which he evidently did not want. Miss Ingelow, in a bonnet and shawl, with a lace veil over her face (it was a garden party), seemed to be stricken with a kind of English shyness which made her rather unresponsive, so that he went away without having been introduced to any one, while every one looked on and wanted to know him.

"I remember an enthusiastic American girl who was introduced to Thomas Hardy by Mrs. Moulton, at one of her Fridays, who exclaimed, 'O Mr. Hardy, to meet you makes this a red letter day for me'; whereupon the quiet, reserved, great man looked at her in speechless alarm and fled. It was at Mrs. Moulton's that I first became acquainted with the editor of the famous 'Yellow Book.' He was Henry Harland, and its publisher was John Lane. I recall Mrs. Moulton saying

'Now that I have introduced the editor to you I must also introduce the publisher.'

"It was in the 'Yellow Book' that the most distinguished of the younger English writers first won their spurs, and that erratic genius, Aubrey Beardsley, made his undying mark on the black and white art, not only of England, but of the world. It was all these younger men whose talent Mrs. Moulton made known to the American public.

"In the first years of my friendship with Mrs. Moulton, when she still wrote fiction, she once told me of the plot of a story which had been told to her by Philip Marston. It was a wonderful plot and Mr. Marston wished her to use it. As she told me the details in her vivid way, I was profoundly impressed as if it had been a story of De Maupassant. She seemed to have no great desire to use it, although she was, for the moment, fired by my young enthusiasm for it. If ever I envied, as only a young literary aspirant can, it was Mrs. Moulton then as the ownership of that plot, and I told her so. 'If I do not use it,' she said, 'I will give it to you.' So years passed, and in my mind still lingered the remembrance of that wonderful plot which, so far, Mrs. Moulton had not used. One evening we were at the theatre together, and as we sat talking, between the acts, she suddenly reverted to the plot. 'I have decided,' she said, 'that I shall never use it, and I will give it to you.' I do not think that any gift ever made me so happy; it was a happiness that only a writer of stories can appreciate. It seemed to me as if I could not find words to express my gratitude for her great generosity. I know my delight made her happy. It was so a part of her to be happy in another's happiness. For days and weeks afterward I only lived in that wonderful plot — but to this day the wonderful plot has not been used."

The numbers of autograph copies of books presented to Mrs. Moulton by their authors she left, by memorandum, to the Boston Public Library, with the request that Professor Arlo Bates make the selection. These now form a memorial collection, each volume marked by a book-plate bearing an engraved portrait of Mrs. Moulton. Professor Bates has written an account of this collection, which, as it has not before been published, may be included here as not only interesting from the inscriptions which it contains, but as indicating the range and variety of Mrs. Moulton's literary friendships.

THE MOULTON COLLECTION

"From the library of Mrs. Louise Chandler Moulton it has been my task — sombre yet grateful — to select a collection of autographed books and first editions to be given to the Public Library of Boston as a Memorial. Between eight and nine hundred volumes were found worthy, and of these no small number are of rarity and much interest. Mrs. Moulton had not only the books presented to her personally by the writers, but from the library of Philip Bourke Marston she inherited many others enriched by the autographs of famous men and women. The list is too long to be given in anything like entirety, but it included Thomas Bailey Aldrich, Mathilde Blind, Frederick von Bodenstedt, Charles Bradlaugh, Alice Brown, Madison Cawein, F. B. Money-Coutts, John Davidson, Austin Dobson, W. H. Drummond, Eugene Field, Richard Garnett, Richard Watson Gilder, Robert Grant, Edmund Gosse, Louise Imogen Guiney, Thomas Wentworth Higginson, H. Rider Haggard, John Hay, William Ernest Henley, Oliver Wendell Holmes, Lord Houghton, Henry James, Amy Levy, Lady Lindsay, Frederick Locker, James Russell Lowell,

FACSIMILE OF BOOK PLATE FROM THE MEMORIAL COLLECTION OF
THE BOOKS OF LOUISE CHANDLER MOULTON
BOSTON PUBLIC LIBRARY

Page 282

Stéphane Mallarmé, Joaquin Miller, George
Moore, Felix Moscheles, the Hon. Roden
Noel, Thomas Nelson Page, John Payne,
Nora Perry, Mr. and Mrs. James B. Piatt,
James Whitcomb Riley, Amélie Rives, C.
G. D. Roberts, Christina Rossetti, William
Sharp, Harriet Prescott Spofford, Edmund
Clarence Stedman, Algernon Charles Swin-
burne, Bayard Taylor, John T. Trowbridge,
Mrs. Humphry Ward, William Watson, Theo-
dore Watts-Dunton, John Greenleaf Whittier,
and Mary Wilkins.

"The exact number of authors represented
has not been counted, but probably the autographed volumes, of which there are about
six hundred, do not contain more than a
fifth of that number of well-known names.
Some signatures are by unknown authors
who sent their books to Mrs. Moulton because
of her prominence; and in a limited number
of cases such have been thrown out as obvi-
ously not worthy of a place in the collection.
The variety of the personal acquaintances
among distinguished writers, however, illustrates very strikingly the breadth of Mrs.
Moulton's sympathies and the remarkable
extent to which she kept in touch with current literature. In not a few cases, moreover, the inscriptions show how often her

encouragement or wise counsel had been helpful to the writer. In 'The White Sail,' Miss Guiney writes: 'To Louise Chandler Moulton from her lover and debtor'; Charles Bradlaugh, in 'The Impeachment of the House of Brunswick': 'From the author to his critic'; F. B. Money-Coutts, in 'King Arthur': 'A poor return for her kind interest'; John Davidson, in 'New Ballads': 'From her obliged friend.' Others of this sort might be quoted, and while dedicatory inscriptions are not always to be taken too seriously, no one could know Mrs. Moulton and her helpful kindliness without realizing to how many writers her sympathetic criticism and judicious advice had been of marked value. C. W. Dalmon, in a copy of the limited edition of 'Song-Favors' writes: 'To Mrs. Louise Chandler Moulton for her kindness' sake, and for the sake of "Philip, our King"; and the remembrance of that kindness in so many hearts is to Mrs. Moulton a lasting monument.'

"From the many and varied inscriptions in these books I have selected a handful which seem to me interesting, and which Mrs. Moulton's friends will, I hope, find so. In going over the library I was struck with the range in time which these autographs cover. It gave a feeling of being in touch with a past

almost that of our grandmothers' to come
upon Le Tellier's '*L'Histoire Ancienne*' with
the inscription: 'Louise Chandler Moulton
from Madame Emma Willard, Troy Female
Seminary, May 30th, 1856'; or upon 'Lucy
Howard's Journal,' bearing upon the fly-leaf:
'Mrs. Ellen Louise Moulton, with the love of
her friend, L. H. Sigourney, Hartford, Conn't.
Christmas, 1857.' The latter volume is dated
by the publishers 1858, so that the trick of
making the title-page state its age with feminine inexactness is less recent than is generally
supposed. Who to-day knows anything about
Madame Willard, or has other remembrance
of Mrs. Sigourney than that of seeing her
name attached to moralizing selections in
the reading-books of our remote youth?

"Older still than these, although the fact
that Mr. Trowbridge has happily been with
us to the present time makes him seem less
a figure of the past, are the inscriptions in
the first and second series of Emerson's
'Essays': 'Ella Louise from Paul Creyton,
April 10th, 1854'; 'To Ellen Louise from
J. T. T., April 10th, 1854.' To the same
year belongs a copy of 'Mrs. Partington,'
in which is written: 'To my granddaughter,
Ellen Louise, Ruth Partington by B. P.
Shillaber.' I confess to something of a wist-

ful feeling at these reminders of a time in
the midyears of a century already dead,
when I was in the nursery and 'Ellen Louise,'
'Paul Creyton,' and 'Mrs. Partington' were
the literary stars glimmering out with yet
ungauged power in the sky where Emerson
and Whittier and Longfellow were the fixed
and shining lights.

" The autographed books, for the most part,
however, belong to the years since Mrs.
Moulton had won her place as the leading
woman-poet of America. Her intimate connection with the literary world in England
has brought it about that almost as many
English as American names are found written on the fly-leaves of presentation copies.
Largely, of course, the sentiments are simple
expressions of regard or admiration, and it
has not seemed worth while to include these
here. Of those which are more full or less
conventional the following are examples: Oswald Crawfurd has written in his 'Portugal':
'My friends consider this my best work, and
if they are right it is the fittest present I can
give to Mrs. Chandler Moulton, the best
friend this year, 1887, has brought me.' In
the 1896 edition of 'Dawn' the author says:
'To Mrs. Chandler Moulton with the kind
regards of H. Rider Haggard. P. S.   Her

appreciation of this old "three-decker," which he remembers working very hard over, has pleased its antiquated author very much indeed, as he imagined that nowadays it only possessed a prehistoric interest.' In Lloyd Mifflin's 'The Fields of Dawn' is written: 'You who know so well — by having so often encountered them yourself — the almost insuperable difficulties of the sonnet form, will be among the first to pardon the many shortcomings of this little volume'; and in 'The Slopes of Parnassus' are quoted with graceful modesty the lines of Tennyson:

> " For though its faults were thick as dust
> In vacant chambers, I could trust
> Your kindness.

Nothing could be more graceful than the inscription of Arthur Sherburne Hardy: 'If the *salut* Passe Rose sang to Queen Hildegarde (p. 354) had not already been verified for you, I should repeat it here. Faithfully yours, etc.' The *salut*, as those will remember who are as fond of 'Passe Rose' as I am, was:

> " God give thee joy,
> And great honor.

In her 'Brownies and Boggles' Miss Guiney has written:

> " ' Of Brownyes and of Boggles fulle is this Beuk.
> GAWAIN DOUGLAS, 1474–1522.

For the "Fairy" Godmother, from her chronicler of elves. L. I. G.' And in 'Goose-Quill Papers': 'To your most gracious hands these weeds and tares.' Clyde Fitch, in a copy of 'The Knighting of the Twins,' mounted from newspaper slips and bound by the author: 'Sweet singer — friendship is a blue, blue sky,— fair, ethereal, interminable, with an horizon made goldy with the sun of love. And your friendship — is a sky still more precious, a heavenly one.' Harriet Prescott Spofford inscribes 'An Inheritance,' 'My dear Louise, with the love of her Hal,' and in turn Mrs. Moulton herself writes in a volume of Mrs. Spofford's 'Poems': 'To Philip Bourke Marston I give these poems of a woman whom I love.' Mrs. Clara Erskine Clement in 'Angels in Art': 'Alas! My pen was not "dropped from an angel's wing," but such things as it writ I send thee with my love.' In a copy of 'Berries of the Briar' I found with amused surprise, as I had not seen it for twenty years or so: 'Louise Chandler Moulton with Christmas greeting from The Briar, 1886.

> " ' Small worth claims my book
>   Save the greeting it brings you.
> I pray you o'erlook
> Small worth. Claims my book

> But that you deign to brook
>   Its intrusion, in view
> That no worth claims my book
>   Save the greeting it brings you.'

Anybody could easily place this sort of verse without a date, for at that time, in the eighties, experiments in French forms were notoriously in fashion. In 'Love Lyrics,' in clear, incisive text one reads: 'For Mrs. Louise Chandler Moulton these humble lines — herein gathered by another than the author's hand — so doubly poor an exchange for her volume of real poetry entitled "At the Wind's Will." With all hale greetings of your ever grateful friend, James Whitcomb Riley. Christmas of 1899.

> " ' *At the Wind's Will!* — So sail these songs of thine
>   Into the haven of hearts — the world's and mine —
> While anchoring-chant of crew and pilot saith:
>   The Wind's will — yea, the will of God's own breath.'

"In 'The World Beautiful' was inscribed: 'To Mrs. Louise Chandler Moulton, whose graciousness and charm create a World Beautiful wherever she goes, this little book is offered, with grateful love.' Dr. Holmes' inscription is a copy of his well-known stanza: 'And if I should live to be.' Edmund Clarence Stedman inscribes his 'Poems': 'To my loyal, lifelong friend, Louise Chandler Moulton, Poet, with love and homage. E. C. Stedman, Thanksgiving, 1897.

> " ' The Power that arches heaven's orbway round
> Gave to this planet's brood its soul of fire;
> Its heart of passion, — and for life unbound
> By chain or creed the measureless desire. — p. 126.'

"The 'American Anthology' three years later has: 'To my life-long, loyalest woman friend — my sister in life and song — Louise Chandler Moulton. Meet whom we may, no others comprehend save those who breathed the same air and drank the same waters when we trod the sunrise fields of Youth.' In 'The Poet's Chronicle,' privately printed in an edition of forty-four copies on Van Gelder paper, is written: 'My old friend, Louise Chandler Moulton, this piece not aimed at the public. Frederick Wedmore, 3rd July, 1902.' 'Heartsease and Rue' Mr. Lowell presents 'to Mrs. Louise Chandler Moulton with the kind regards of the author, who wishes her all heartsease and no rue.' In this volume, as in a number of others, a signed letter is inserted, either one which accompanied the gift in the first place or which replied to the acknowledgment of the recipient. 'Astrophel and Other Poems' is sent 'To Mrs. Moulton from A. C. Swinburne in memoriam Philip Bourke Marston.'

"Among the Marston books are many of interest, but of them I have space to mention only two. One is a copy of 'Ecce Homo,' to 'Philip Bourke Marston from his god-mother, D. M. C., Aug. 13, 1866.' Dinah Mulock Craik's poem to her godson, 'Philip, my King,' is well known, and is alluded to in one of the inscriptions which I have already quoted. Mr. Marston's godfather, Philip James Bailey, bestowed upon him a copy of 'Festus,' with the inscription: *'Ce livre donné affectueusement par l'auteur à son cher filleul Philippe Bourke Marston, qui a déja par son propre genie étendue la renommée patronymique, est accompagné des voeux les plus sincères pour la santé et pour son bonheur."* Just why French should be used in this connection is not evident, and perhaps I am not justified in feeling that 'Festus' Bailey was perhaps not without a secret pride in being able to achieve an inscription in that language. Be that as it may, however, the sentiment expressed is a graceful one, not ungracefully put. The third volume is a copy of Swinburne's 'A Song of Italy.' In it is this note: 'This copy was read by Mr. Swinburne, on March 30th, 1867, to Mr. Mazzini, and has been in the hand of the great Italian to whom it is dedicated. Presented to Philip

Bourke Marston by Thomas Purnell, 12 April, 1867.'

"I have already much exceeded the limits within which in beginning this paper I meant to end. I have therefore no space in which to speak of the first and limited editions or of the privately printed books which add to the value of the collection. It is to me a source of much satisfaction that this fine and dignified memorial to Mrs. Moulton should be in the Public Library of Boston. The bookplate by Sidney L. Smith contains her portrait, and a catalogue of the books has been printed. Mrs. Moulton's work is her monument, but this will be an appropriate and fitting recognition of her place in American letters and in the gracious company of New England's poets."

The autograph letters left by Mrs. Moulton, the greater number written to her personally but some which were well-nigh priceless (like the original of the famous letter in which Mrs. Browning stated her view of spiritualism) from the bequest of Mr. Marston, were carefully assorted, and by her daughter given to the Congressional Library at Washington. To them was added the large number of autographed photographs which Mrs. Moulton had received as gifts from famous or distinguished persons.

The place of Louise Chandler Moulton as a writer is assured. The words of the *London Athenæum* in its memorial notice may be said to sum up the matter with entire justice when it said that her work "entitles her to her recognized position as the first poet, among women," in America, from the fact that her verse possesses "delicate and rare beauty, marked originality, and, what was better still, . . . a sense of vivid and subtle imagination, and that spontaneous feeling which is the essence of lyrical poetry." Her mastery of the sonnet-form has been commented upon in the words of critics of authority a number of times already in this volume, and neither this nor her wonderful instinct for metrical effect need be dwelt upon here. That she has left her place in American letters unfilled, and that no successor is in evidence will hardly be disputed. Few writers of equal eminence have so completely escaped from all trace of mannerism, for unless a tendency to melancholy might be so classed her poetry is unusually free from this fault. The imaginative spontaneity of her verse made it impossible for artificiality to intrude; and even the sadness never seems forced or affected. The beauty of feeling and the exquisite melody of her verse have in them the savor of immortality.

To her friends the remembrance of her genius for friendship, — for it amounted to that, — her wonderful and unworldly kindness which overflowed in all her acts, the sympathy which no demands could exhaust, must seem hardly less a title to continued remembrance than her poetic powers. Her life was singularly complete, singularly fortunate, in its conditions. It was a life enriched with genius, friendship, and love, and above all it was the life of one whose nature was golden throughout with the appreciation of beauty and the instinctive generosity which gave as freely as it had received.

She had entered into the larger life where

No work begun shall ever pause for death,

and where all the nobler energies of the spirit shall enter into eternal beauty.